The Energy Solution

A Mother's Guide to go from Frazzled and Fatigued to Full of Life

Teressa Todd

First published by Busybird Publishing 2018
Copyright © 2018 Teressa Todd

ISBN
Print: 978-1-925830-45-3
Ebook: 978-1-925830-62-0

Teressa Todd has asserted her right under the Copyright, Designs and Patents Act 1988 to be identified as the author of this work. The information in this book is based on the author's experiences and opinions. The publisher specifically disclaims responsibility for any adverse consequences, which may result from use of the information contained herein. Permission to use information has been sought by the author. Any breaches will be rectified in further editions of the book.

All rights reserved. No part of this publication may be reproduced, stored in or introduced into a retrieval system, or transmitted in any form, or by any means (electronic, mechanical, photocopying, recording or otherwise) without the prior written permission of the author. Any person who does any unauthorised act in relation to this publication may be liable to criminal prosecution and civil claims for damages. Enquiries should be made through the publisher.

Cover image: Busybird Publishing
Cover design: Busybird Publishing
Layout and typesetting: Busybird Publishing

Busybird Publishing
2/118 Para Road
Montmorency, Victoria
Australia 3094
www.busybird.com.au

DISCLAIMER:

This book and its content are for informational purposes only and are intended to assist the reader to help identify symptoms and health challenges. It is not intended to be a substitute for medical advice of a qualified medical professional.

Testimonials

I have experienced a number of immune disorders that had left me with chronic fatigue and autoimmune diseases. They were painful and debilitating, and I suffered greatly from a variety of symptoms. Teressa was able identify the triggers and through live blood microscopy, assess what was happening in my body. She then provided a treatment plan that used natural ingredients, with nutritional guidance and beneficial lifestyle changes that provided me a pathway for self-healing and wellness again.

Jenny S

Teressa came highly recommended, and I certainly arrived at her clinic in a bit of a mess. I was years into a chronic fatigue diagnosis, had nursed a lifetime of gut sensitivities and was in a horrible pattern of picking up every virus going around. I was struck by a number of things at my first appointment – Teressa's calm approach, intuition and systematic way of dealing with my abundance of issues. What could have been completely overwhelming, wasn't. She sorted issues out one by one and explained everything along the way.

At the six-month mark my improvement was undeniable; at nine months, remarkable; at a year, permanent. Life changing is an understatement – I now have consistent energy, immunity and understand how to care for my gut.

Tina T

In my early 30s I became ill. I went from being a party girl and working 70 hours a week to not being able to lift my head off the pillow. I couldn't stay awake and was sleeping 20 hours a day. I didn't have the energy to speak. My brain stopped working and I had complete brain fog. I was working full-time as well as studying computer science full-time, and suddenly everything stopped working. I was suffering from chronic fatigue syndrome (CFS).

Teressa is a phenomenon at diagnostics and within the first session was able to pinpoint what the issues were and gave me simple, logical, easy to follow advice. It didn't happen overnight, but as I changed my lifestyle and the bad habits that had caused the illness, the damage was reversed and my body healed itself. Now 20 years on, I live by the fundamentals Teressa discussed with me in that first session, and if I start to feel the CFS symptoms start to return I would go back to the basics to get back on track. Thank goodness for Teressa … I am eternally grateful to her and thankful that she does what she does.

Kathryn H

We are so grateful to have Teressa in our lives and our whole family goes twice a year for our regular health checks. I have referred everyone I know who has any health issues to Teressa and they all come back to me saying thank you for sending them to Teressa. She is an amazing healer and will fix your issues. Give it a go, what have you got to lose? Please remember healing is a process, it takes time and if you give Teressa that time, she will have you feeling better than you ever have before.

I am so pleased to have her in our lives and I admire her professionalism and determination to find the answer to any health issue. She is incredible and I am proud to know her.

Tracey C

As I have a gardening business, my body needs to keep up with a busy pace. Teressa has shown me the way to do this, her constant reminders of good nutrition, naturopathic remedies and blood screening has been essential to keeping a good health regime.

My daughter's energy and health also improved dramatically with Teressa's guidance.

A big thank you to Teressa from both of us.
 Linda B

Teressa, thank you for fixing my immune system. I went straight through winter without a virus while working in a school where I talk to students most of the day and where at least three staff have been off each day for the past several weeks. I would go as far as saying my immune system is better than before I had glandular fever – thanks to you.
 Sue M

When I came to Teressa my body was completely exhausted both physically and mentally. After years of functioning but not really living, I came to realise that not only did I have to improve my dietary habits but change my thought about healthy living through a combined effort of body, mind and learning to respect my body. I am now very conscious of feeding my body healthy foods and supplements and even started growing some of my own vegetables! I have felt improvements and know that with your continued help, I am heading towards a more energised and healthy future.
 Susan C

Dedication

I dedicate this book to several key people in my life.

Firstly, to my husband, Peter, who is my best friend and soul mate. You are an amazing and resilient man that will not let a chronic health situation drag you down. Your strength is admirable. I thank you for supporting me through this.

To my children, Sienna and Caylem, you are the loves of my life and I love sharing life's experiences with you and watching you flourish.

To my late mother, thank you for your guidance and support in helping me become the person I am today. Also, to my mother-in-law, you have been a second mum to me over the years. Thank you for your love and support.

I wish to thank all my clients over the 20+ years of clinical practice who have entrusted me with your health journey. You have shown me your strength and ability for amazing change.

Contents

Prelude	i
1. Activate Your Digestion	1
2. Recharge Your Liver	9
3. Clarify Your Kidneys	25
4. Power Up Your Adrenals and Thyroid	33
5. Hormone Chaos	47
6. Stealth Infections	59
7. Energy Robbers	69
8. Magic Herbs and Nutrients	81
9. Sleep Easy Solutions	97
10. Recharge ME	107
11. Game Plan	117
12. Take Control	127
Afterword	137
Offers	139
About the Author	141

Prelude

Did You Skip Breakfast?

If your answer is 'yes', then it is likely that you want to skip reading the introduction to this book. I encourage you to read this, stop and think about what else you are skipping in your day, your week or your life. What are you forgoing for you?

This book, *The Energy Solution*, came about because many of my clients came to see me to address their tiredness and fatigue. Many felt they were skipping life. Over the years, a majority of these clients have been mothers, and I have seen a trend of mothers doing so much in their life that they don't have time to stop and recharge. They keep pushing themselves to take on so many responsibilities. The mothers get sick from an infection but have a need to keep going to tend to the family and to their work, they don't allow themselves time to recover fully.

The current era of mothers are juggling many roles, doing many tasks each day and feeling the need to push themselves through the day. It has been described as the advent of the 'Supermum'.

There are now 'mumpreneurs', mums who work full-time, single mums, and mums who are dealing with major stressful events in their lives. All these women tend to burn the candle at both ends and push through fatigue daily to continue to be there for their loved ones, bosses, friends and family.

Looking at health and energy is like looking at a puzzle. Within a puzzle there are many pieces that make up the whole picture. The same can be said about health. There are many reasons – or puzzle pieces – that cause fatigue and ill-health. It is about identifying those puzzle pieces and putting them together to get the whole picture of health.

This book is written in a form, and an order, that addresses each piece of the puzzle. Let us address the issues in each of the chapters to supercharge your health and find the pieces of the puzzle for your fatigue. It may be just one reason, or puzzle piece, that is causing your fatigue. More often than not, I find it is a combination of reasons that cause fatigue and imbalance, for example, a combination of nutrition and thyroid dysfunction can cause fatigue.

By implementing the information in each of the chapters, you can take charge of your health and restore your energy and vitality. This book is not meant to be heavily scientific. It is written to give you an easy yet informed understanding of how the body works so that you can take control of your health.

In the first few chapters I give a description about the body systems and how they work. This is to help you understand the *why* of what is happening, so you can take action towards your own health. Having a well-informed understanding will also give you more reason to change and stick with the changes, rather than a surface knowledge that leads you to half-hearted efforts. This is your health and your life. Live it well.

For many women, they are so rushed and have so much to do constantly that their body cannot keep up with this lifestyle. Our body is not designed for the speed and demand of the current world. It is important that we take steps to protect our body and that we take time out for ourselves to rest, recuperate and recharge.

Why Are Things Different Now?

Women in previous generations didn't have the speed and number of roles that the current era of women have. The technology age means that everyone is plugged in constantly. We are inundated with stimuli. As women, we find it hard to turn off.

Our grandparents had an entirely different lifestyle. I have listened to my grandmother and mother talk of a time when they had no electricity and therefore no telephone or internet. Life was simpler without constant interruption from technology and the 24/7 demands of today's world. In the era prior to advanced technology, if you didn't want to be contacted, you would have just taken the phone off the hook or go for a walk without a mobile phone in hand (as there were none). Furthermore, food was grown in the local area and free of many additives found in today's processed foods.

I'm not saying their life in those times didn't have stresses and demands, it just didn't seem to have the same intensity experienced by the modern woman today.

Looking at how the human body is designed, our genetics haven't changed much over the thousands of years, but the environment we live in has changed dramatically. The responsibilities of the tribal woman during prehistoric hunter-gatherer times revolved around daily activities to stay alive, such as gathering and preparing food and reproducing and rearing children. The tribal woman lived in an untainted, nature-based environment and they ate food as nature provided. They lived and ate by the seasons and went to sleep and woke up with the sun.

The responsibilities of the woman in the current era is much more. The environment we now live in consists of closely built housing, pollution from cars, very little nature time, food that is processed and at times doesn't even resemble anything that is provided by nature, and a lifestyle that is relatively inactive. We don't follow the seasons or the earth's rhythms, we use artificial light during darkness to stay up late doing more tasks to catch up from the day after the kids have gone to bed. We cram as much as we can into each and every day, without much downtime or relaxation time.

We expect so much more from our bodies in this modern world. The chemical reactions of the body that drive health and energy production are just not keeping up with the demand.

Why Is Fatigue So Prevalent?

Fatigue is a symptom that can be due to many different reasons. It can stand alone as a single symptom or it can be part of a chronic disease or illness. To conquer fatigue, we need to look at the possible reasons for it and address each of them. This book is here to help women identify them and then make changes to move toward a better state of health.

Factors that contribute to fatigue include poor food selection and poor nutrition, incorrect eating patterns, overload of our filters, viral, bacterial or parasitic infections, mental and emotional pressures, and sheer overload of duties. One alone can be significant but many modern-day mums are juggling multiple factors and still expect themselves to continue daily life with abundance.

As mums we deal with many expectations on a daily basis. Sometimes these expectations can come from external parties such as friends, family or bosses. On the other hand, majority of the time it will come from within ourselves.

I am a mother, wife, homemaker, financier, clinical health provider, business owner and income provider. I understand the many hats that women must wear and still try to muster enough energy and vitality to keep up with our children and maintain a happy home life.

As a clinical naturopath, I support many clients through their own fatigue and health issues. That doesn't mean that I am exempt from the issues that trigger fatigue and feelings of overwhelm. I have experienced fatigue throughout my life due to a thyroid condition.

Currently I have a delightful role as a mum to two beautiful children, aged five and nine, as well as a loveable Spoodle. I am also a wife to a wonderful man who has multiple sclerosis – a chronic health condition that affects the central nervous system.

Everyone has situations that create stress and demand on them. There have been a couple of times that my husband has fallen quite ill as a result of the condition. Don't get me wrong, he is doing well considering the fact, but there have been hiccups in his health over the last few years. During these times, I felt an immense emotional burden, as you would when you see a loved one suffer.

At times when I found the circumstances quite demanding, instead of just being in the situation, I would place extra pressure on myself. My thoughts became almost fully consumed with how I would make sure that I could provide emotionally, physically, mentally and financially for my husband and children. Although I tried to concentrate on changing my thoughts and creating a positive environment to live in, the negative thoughts that were going on constantly in my head would consume me.

Negative thoughts in our subconscious creates a stress response and influence our genetics to create specific chemical reactions. For the last few years I have had to heed my own advice that I gave to my clients and work on maintaining a positive, healthy, nutrition-filled environment to work and live in. I cannot change the situations that are occurring, but I can take control of how I live and thrive in this environment.

My goal with this book is to help you get through your daily grind and optimise your health and well-being so that you can truly live your life to the fullest and enjoy your time with your loved ones.

Let's go on a journey together to discover the pieces of your puzzle. In order to complete the puzzle and gain the wholesome picture of a healthy life, let us find out how our body functions and reacts, the importance of specific nutrients, as well as unravel the impact of thoughts and the key principles of health and vitality.

By becoming vital and fabulous, you can help create a world of mums that are no longer tired or fatigued, and we can all show our children and others how to thrive in the current fast-paced environment. This will happen when we understand and listen to our bodies to follow our health path.

1. Activate Your Digestion

'Chewing your food thoroughly and in a relaxed way is the key to optimum nutrition and energy.'

– Teressa Todd

The human body is a wondrous apparatus. I have been working with the human body for over twenty years and yet I am still in admiration of its efficiency and how all its systems work together. Every day we are exposed to a myriad of chemicals, foods, toxins and by-products which these systems can help filter out.

Our body protects us from the countless number of chemicals through various filter systems. These filters include the digestive system, liver and kidneys. When your filters are overloaded, toxins accumulate in your body leaving you feeling tired, fatigued, emotional, unmotivated, moody, stressed and generally just not quite right. Many clients come to me and say, 'I just don't feel right. There's nothing wrong medically, but I just don't feel right.'

In this chapter I will reveal how your filters are vital to the energy production of your body, what happens when they become overwhelmed, and how fatigue can set in when they are neglected.

When your filters are functioning properly, you will feel happier, less stressed, less emotional and more balanced. You will feel like you're more capable of enjoying everyday life. There will also be less brain fog and you will be able to make clearer and faster decisions.

Digestion – The First Filter

Let's talk about digestion. When you think of digesting your food, what comes to mind? We eat food, it goes in our mouth and it goes through a few tubes in the body and comes out the other end, right?

Let's break down the digestion process to show you how a lack of correct functioning can contribute to your fatigue. The process of digestion is to take nutrients in, so that your body can convert these nutrients into energy for use by the body.

If you can't digest your food properly, then you can't get the nutrients from the food.

NO Nutrients = NO Energy

The process of digestion starts before you put the food in your mouth. Firstly, you hear the food, see it, and smell it. The senses tell the brain that food is on the way. The brain sends a message to the stomach to start producing stomach acid ready to digest the food. If you are constantly rushing and you grab a sandwich from a fridge to eat at your work desk or grab a drive-through meal from a fast food chain to eat 'on-the-run', then the brain doesn't get the signal to the stomach in time to create the adequate digestive enzymes and acids.

When this happens, you cannot break your food down adequately to extract the proper nutrients, leaving you nutritionally depleted and beginning the road to fatigue.

What Happens During Digestion?

Digestion is an intricate set of chemical reactions that starts with the mechanical process of chewing your food. You put the food in your mouth and your teeth chew the food up into smaller pieces. The smaller particles of food mix with saliva and enzymes of the mouth allowing the starch content (a form of carbohydrate) of the food to break down further. About a third of your starch carbohydrate digestion occurs in your mouth.

Saliva has a necessary function in the digestion process, it acts as a lubricant for the food to be able to pass down easier through the oesophagus and into the stomach. In the current time of busyness and overwhelm, there is a tendency to be too busy to chew food thoroughly. Many almost inhale their food, chewing only once or twice before it's swallowed in large gulps. This does not help the digestive system's ability to release the nutrients from that food.

Chewing is an undervalued process. The reasons for chewing are something that I spend time discussing with many of my clients as part of their health journey. Chewing is not just about breaking the food into smaller particles for easier swallowing. It is necessary to help the brain send a message to the stomach, signalling for stomach acid to be produced; and if you don't chew your foods thoroughly and allow the saliva to mix with the food, then nutrient absorption can be limited. For instance, vitamin B12 cannot be absorbed properly if it doesn't mix with key elements of the saliva. Vitamin B12 is vital for energy, brain and nervous system.

Once the food is broken down by the teeth into smaller particles and has passed through the oesophagus to the stomach, the acids and the enzymes of the stomach interact with the food particles and continue to break down the particles into their smallest units. Think of chewing in terms of getting gold that is trapped inside a quartz rock. To release the gold, you need to break apart the quartz using a physical force. The nutrients in your food cannot be released until you break down the food into its smallest units using the chewing action.

Once the chewed food is in the stomach, it needs to be broken down further by stomach acid and enzymes called pepsin and lipase. These enzymes break down some of the protein and the fats. The acidity level of the stomach acid needs to be at pH 2 in order to break apart the food particles into smaller parts. If the body is stressed or the signal from the brain has not had enough time to send the message to the stomach, then the acidity level will not be low enough for proper digestion. When your stomach acidity and enzymes are not sufficient, you can feel bloated and tired after eating a meal.

Once the food leaves the stomach, it moves into the small intestine where the liver and pancreas inject more enzymes to continue the breakdown of the carbohydrates, protein and fats into their smallest units. Only then can the vital nutrients be absorbed and transported across the intestinal membrane. If you haven't broken down the food properly, you cannot absorb and transport those small molecule nutrients across into your bloodstream to be used by the body for energy production and health.

This is why it's vital to get the first couple of phases of digestion occurring properly, that is chewing your food and being thorough in the process of breaking the food down from large size to smaller sizes. If any part of this process is not properly done, you will suffer from low energy, lack of nutrients and lack of key elements to create cellular energy and repair.

How's Your Digestion?

Here is a questionnaire for you to find out if your digestive system is not functioning optimally.

1. Activate Your Digestion

Tick the symptoms that relate to you:

- ❑ Excessive burping or belching
- ❑ Bad breath
- ❑ Burning sensation in chest, reflux or heartburn
- ❑ Bloating during or immediately after meals
- ❑ Bloating for several hours after eating
- ❑ Sensation of fullness for hours after meals
- ❑ Flatulence or excessive wind
- ❑ Food intolerances

- ☐ Abdominal cramping
- ☐ Feeling tired immediately after meals
- ☐ Loss of appetite
- ☐ Nausea after eating
- ☐ Constipation
- ☐ Diarrhoea
- ☐ Alternating between constipation and diarrhoea
- ☐ Sensation of incomplete bowel movements
- ☐ Undigested food in stools
- ☐ Variable colour of stools

Add up the number of boxes you ticked.

If you scored 7 or more, you may have poor digestion function. This can be contributing to your fatigue and tiredness.

How to Improve Your Digestion

1. Take your time when you eat in order to chew your food thoroughly. Avoid eating quickly and simply swallowing your food after two bites. Many of my clients are time poor and eat while working in front of their computer or at their work desk. If you do this, you will not be aware of whether you are chewing your food or just swallowing it. Put your knife, fork and spoon down between your bites and think about the tastes in your mouth, this will help encourage you to chew your food thoroughly.

2. Avoid eating mindlessly. What do I mean by this? Turn off your television, put aside your mobile phone, and set aside your computer. Be present while you eat your meal. Savour

the flavours and the textures of the food you're eating. Create almost a ritual with the eating process. Believe me, your food deserves the love and attention from you, the same way you deserve the nutrition it provides you.

3. As a young child I came from a religious family and we had to give thanks for the food we were about to receive. It was the beginning of the meal process before we ate, and as a child I hated it. Now as an adult, I can see that the concept of being thankful for what the food will do for my health should start off the eating process for any meal. Be aware and thankful for what this food will do for you and the nourishment that it will provide you.

4. When you're aware while eating your meal and you're chewing slower, you will be less likely to overeat and that can help with weight problems. Similarly, by eating slower and chewing your food thoroughly, you are less likely to feel bloated and will be able to skip that post-meal tiredness.

5. Use apple cider vinegar or lemon juice to help stimulate the digestive process. I recommend to my clients to take two tablespoons of apple cider vinegar or lemon juice mixed in a small amount of water about five to ten minutes before their meals. This can help boost the process of the brain instructing the stomach that there is food on the way and to start creating that digestive acids and enzymes needed.

6. Limit drinking with your meals. Excess fluid can dilute your stomach's acidity, depending upon they type of drink it is. Alkaline water has been popular lately, but unfortunately, when taken with meals it will alter the acidity of your stomach and prevent you from being able to digest food properly. Soft drinks and alcohol can also inhibit digestion. Stop drinking thirty minutes before a meal and wait at least

one hour after the meal to have a drink. Simply enjoy the food that comes with the meal.

7. Add spices and herbs to your meal. While they can add a lot of flavour to your dishes, spices and herbs can also help stimulate your digestion. Culinary herbs and spices such as ginger, black pepper, turmeric, cayenne, coriander, cardamom, cumin, peppermint, fennel, cinnamon, basil, thyme and dill can help promote your digestion. These herbs and spices can help to stimulate the digestive enzymes, enhance absorption of nutrients and soothe the digestive tract. Ayurvedic culture reveres spices and herbs as part of its medicinal approach.

8. If you are struggling with digestion and have a lot of the symptoms from the list above, then you may need help to restore your digestive balance. Meadowsweet, Gentian, Schisandra, Oregon Grape, Ginger and Yarrow are just some of the herbs that I love to use in a remedy to help my clients. These herbs are best used as an herbal formula before meals to help stimulate digestion. Get some advice from a qualified herbalist to help you select the best herbs for your situation.

Improving your digestive process is key to renewing your life's vitality and vigour. Ensuring that you get adequate nutrition through digestion will allow your body to heal and repair itself, whilst restoring equilibrium. The body is designed to live in a balanced state and will need the right environment – good nutrition resulting from a well-functioning digestion – in order to maintain that balance. Restore your body today and make these changes a part of your daily life.

2. Recharge Your Liver

'The liver handles a myriad of roles everyday – it is essential that you support your liver function. In doing so you will improve your health, energy and vitality.'

– Teressa Todd

The next filter we will look at in respect to your energy and fatigue is the liver. It's the second largest filter of the body and is closely linked to the skin – the largest elimination organ. When the liver is overloaded, excess toxins can be directed to the skin for removal. As these toxins are being eliminated, the skin can become itchy and rashes can present themselves. Itchy skin and rashes can be an indication of your liver becoming overburdened.

The liver is the only internal organ of the body that has been shown to regenerate itself after injury or surgery. We can live with as little as 10% of our liver – live but not thrive. By ensuring the liver is fully functional and has the ability to fulfil its roles, you will be able to thrive.

Roles of the Liver

The liver is a large filter, but that's not its only role. It's fundamentally linked to energy production. Over 500 vital functions have been associated with the liver, some of these are commonly known, and some are performed in combination with other systems of the body. Let's look into them and see how it affects your energy and fatigue.

In the previous section we discussed that nutrients were absorbed through the walls of the intestine. Much of the absorbed material is the nutrition we use, while some absorbed material may be toxic to our system, for example alcohol. All the absorbed material from your stomach and intestines needs to be filtered through the liver first before it goes anywhere else.

The liver filters almost everything that enters the body. While blood transports oxygen and nutrients around the body, it also collects toxins or cell waste from the cells and returns them to the liver. All chemicals will pass through the liver – unwanted nutrients, hormones, microorganisms such as bacteria and viruses, the by-products of the bacteria and viruses, alcohol and neurotransmitters, to name a few.

The liver creates bile which is the carrier that helps to take toxins out of the system. Bile is also important in helping break down the fats that are consumed in a meal. Another role that the liver has is metabolising the carbohydrates and converting excess glucose (or blood sugar) into a storage form called glycogen.

In the current diet, many of us tend to consume a lot of refined sugar when we're tired and run-down, thinking it will help give us energy. Unfortunately, that sugar consumption creates more demand on a liver that is already burdened.

The liver is also a storage organ. It stores nutrients such as fat-soluble vitamins – vitamin A or vitamin D – as well as vitamin B12, iron and copper. There is a genetic condition called haemochromatosis whereby the body absorbs too much iron and then stores it in organs, including the brain, heart and liver. The stored iron can have a detrimental impact on the functioning of the affected organ.

As you can see, the liver has a lot of roles in the body and these are only some of them. When you're feeling tired and fatigued, it could be that the liver is not able to do all these processes in the correct manner. By helping the liver and restoring its functions, we can help boost our energy.

As mums we tend to do a lot of jobs every day and can easily get worn out by them. Consider the plight of the overburdened liver – the food we consume, the hidden sugars in our food, the artificial flavours, colours and preservatives, the fats we consume, the alcohol we drink, the stress chemicals we experience, the chemicals contained in our personal care products and perfumes, the hormones we produce daily or take daily in the form of a contraceptive, the air-conditioning chemicals we breathe in and the radiation that we are exposed to from our digital devices.

I am not being 'Debbie Downer' here, instead it is an example of how the liver is burdened daily and still needs to keep going. When the liver becomes overburdened and the detoxification reactions cannot keep up with the current demand, we are left feeling tired, exhausted and run-down. As an overwhelmed, fatigued mum, you will be able to identify with the demands of the liver.

So how can you help your liver? There are many books on liver cleansing diets and liver cleansing products in health food shops that you can look in to. Liver cleanses are like spring cleaning for your house, many people do this once a year. While it is important to do a liver cleanse regularly, it is more important to look after your liver every day and help to reduce the load on the liver daily, not just once or twice a year.

Is Your Liver Overburdened?

Tick the symptoms that relate to you:

- ❏ Have a bloated or full feeling one hour after a meal
- ❏ Fatty or rich foods cause indigestion and/or nausea
- ❏ Unexplained nausea
- ❏ Sensitive to smells, perfumes and other fragrances
- ❏ Pain under ribs especially on right side
- ❏ Dark circles under eyes
- ❏ Skin issues including acne and dermatitis
- ❏ Unexplained itchy skin

- ❏ Yellow discolouration of skin or eyes
- ❏ Pale clay coloured stools
- ❏ Dark urine and strong smell of urine
- ❏ Fluid retention in legs and ankles
- ❏ Blood sugar imbalances
- ❏ Premenstrual syndrome symptoms such as mood changes, cramps, clotting, sore breasts, acne and sugar cravings
- ❏ Struggle to lose weight
- ❏ Easy bruising
- ❏ Low motivation
- ❏ Irritability and quick to anger
- ❏ Tight muscles
- ❏ Waking up during early hours of the morning (between 1 to 3 am) and struggle to get back to sleep

Add up the number of boxes you ticked.

If you scored 8 or more, your liver may be overburdened and in need of support. The overburdened liver may be causing your fatigue.

Taking Care of Your Overburdened Liver

1. **Reduce the overall toxin load in your food.** Food has a large impact on the liver. The liver needs to be able to regulate our blood sugar levels, metabolise the fats in our foods, and metabolise the myriad of preservatives, colours, flavours and additives added to our foods for convenience and taste.

Much of the food today is manufactured in food production warehouses. Additives such as preservatives are added to give longer shelf life; colours are added to give appeal when looking at them before eating; flavours are added to get us hooked onto the food so we come back again and again to repurchase.

During university, one of my subjects was called Consumer Food. This class was about how we could manipulate the ingredient list to make chemical ingredients sound healthy and use that to market products to the public. We were taught how to hide ingredients from the consumer through labelling. Hence, it is vital that we are aware of what we are buying and be smart and selective about the food we use.

These days I tend to stick to foods that have minimal ingredients and avoid altogether foods that have a number of chemical-looking names. If you want to look at the ingredients that you are putting in your mouth, download *Chemical Maze*, an app that lists ingredients of food and gives you a description of what the ingredient does and how it affects the body. Ingredients that are harmful or potentially harmful are given a yellow or red sad face, and ingredients that are safe for the body are given a green smiley face.

Try to eat as clean or as close to nature as possible. What I mean by this is to eat unprocessed food with little or no additives. Base your meals on salad, fruits and vegetables, with smaller amounts of meats and grains. Keep processed food or fast food to a minimum. Give your liver food as nature intended, the body knows what to do with the food that comes from nature. It doesn't know how to deal with chemicals that came from a laboratory.

2. **Reduce your refined sugar load**. Refined white sugar offers us no nutritional value. In order for our body to process the refined sugar, it uses up vital nutrients such as magnesium, zinc, chromium and B vitamins, and places added demands upon the pancreas and liver. Refined sugar comes in many forms – there are more than sixty different names to identify sugar. Some of these include high fructose corn syrup, sucrose, dextrose, malt syrup, glucose, fructose, maltodextrin and maltose.

   Knowing this, why do we still eat refined white sugar? It is because many of us link the up-front sugar 'high' to energy and think it will help solve our fatigue. At 2 pm when we are flagging in energy at work and need an energy boost, we grab the chocolate bar and feel a brief energy burst. This is then followed by a drastic drop in energy levels about an hour later, just in time for us to pick the kids up from school and race around with after-school activities. This is also the point where we become irritable and cranky. Due to the lag in time we don't correlate the energy low with the sugar rush wearing off.

   I call it the 'sugar roller coaster ride'. One minute we feel up and then the next we are down, looking for the next up again.

   Some clients come to me and say they are avoiding all sugars – even from fruits and vegetables. Sugars from fruits and vegetables are not to blame. Fruits contain many nutrients beneficial to our health and energy production, as well as fibre that blunts the sugar high. It is the refined sugar, and the high sugar load in a lot of our foods – especially low-fat foods – that are placing the load on the liver.

In the afternoon, instead of going for the quick chocolate bar or some other sugar fix, try having a snack that is loaded with good fats and nutrition, such as a handful of activated almonds or macadamias, or some dates. Try a smoothie packed with nutrition from cucumber, berries, hemp seeds, spinach leaves and coconut water with the addition of some brain-empowering avocado. Make your own homemade muesli bar slice with a drizzle of dark cacao chocolate, or carrot cake energy balls.

These snack ideas are all available on my website, *www.teressatodd.com*. Go to resources tab and use code word 'FABULOUS' for access. These snacks will help keep your energy levels more stable, you will feel less irritated and cranky, and your liver will thank you later.

3. **Limit your alcohol.** Many clients use alcohol to relax and unwind at the end of the day. It has become part of the daily habit. You may not want to hear it, but alcohol robs the body of many vital nutrients required for energy production, such as selenium, B vitamins, zinc and magnesium. The liver will have the added job to metabolise alcohol and break it down into another form that can be eliminated from our system.

Alcohol and the sugar in alcohol changes the bacterial levels of our intestines. This bacterial level – also known as the microbiome – is responsible for many health aspects of our body. A change in the microbiome can contribute to fatigue, increase the biotoxin load for the liver to detoxify, leave you foggy in thought, change your ability to deal with stress, and contribute to weight gain. *All this from alcohol?*

Try this: Avoid alcohol for four weeks and take note of your energy. How does your foggy head feel? Are your energy levels more stable? Write down your energy levels on a daily basis during this time and rate your energy on a scale of 1 to 10 with 10 being the highest. At the end of four weeks, go over your energy scale and see the change.

When I discuss this with my clients, some still say that they don't feel they are capable of cutting alcohol consumption despite knowing how it affects their energy and health condition. In this case, I would suggest that, at a minimum, they reduce their alcohol consumption to weekends only. This gives their body four to five days off alcohol per week.

If you do drink and would struggle to stop alcohol for four weeks, then keep a record of how you feel the next day after drinking. Do you wake up groggy? Do you have a restless night's sleep? Are you more irritable the next few days? By keeping a record of how you feel each day, you can see the effects of alcohol on yourself and the pattern that it creates. This can help give you the resolve to make changes in your life for the better.

The next thing to look at is why you are opting to drink alcohol. For many women, they are hungry and tired at the end of the day, grabbing a glass of wine while they make dinner helps to stave off the hunger pangs and helps to settle the overactive mind. Instead, try to have a healthy snack on the way home and a large glass of filtered water before you reach for the alcohol, then see if you still need the alcohol.

Another reason many can relate to is the association between relaxation and alcohol. We pour a glass of wine or spirit and enjoy it while winding down on the sofa at the end of a long day. Try to use another method to unwind before reaching for the bottle. Have some relaxing music playing in the car on the way home or when you get home. Take some time, perhaps ten minutes, to sit and have a cup of tea or a sparkling mineral water with lime while watching the clouds go by outside before you go on with the rest of your day. Taking those ten minutes to unwind for yourself will help to make the difference you are looking for.

4. **Reduce your caffeine intake**. Coffee, strong black teas, Cola and energy drinks create a burden on your liver. Caffeine may be a quick fix when you're tired and run-down, but you then crash a couple of hours later and need another pickup, so it's a rollercoaster ride for you. Caffeine can exacerbate your adrenal imbalance. This is a topic we discuss in the next chapter. But in a nutshell, if you are becoming adrenally fatigued, then caffeine is going to mask it and make it harder to recognise.

Caffeine can increase your symptoms of irritability, nervousness, anxiety, insomnia and digestive issues. After years in the clinic I find that many women are so busy in the morning that they grab a cup of coffee to get them going through the day, and they say it helps them curb the feeling of hunger. Those who skip breakfast miss out on vital nutrients that are needed to help create energy and support optimal health. Instead they end up feeling quite tired and foggy in the afternoon, then they look for the sugar fix to get them through the afternoon.

Caffeinated beverages impede your absorption of minerals, especially magnesium and calcium. These minerals are vital for energy support and brain neurotransmitters to help keep you calm and relaxed. Caffeine contributes to blood sugar level spikes and hence – adding together with existing stress hormones – promote jittery feelings, brain fog, anxiety, shakiness, headaches and irritability.

Cola and energy drinks not only contain caffeine but also introduce other chemicals into the body that the liver needs to metabolise. Some of these chemicals include flavours and sugars or artificial sugars. The liver needs to metabolise these on top of the caffeine influence.

Just as with alcohol, avoiding caffeinated beverages will help to restore your energy. The main issue with cutting caffeine consumption is the withdrawal symptoms and the reliance on the caffeine kick. The symptoms can include headaches, bodily aches and pains, brain fog, dizziness, fatigue, constipation and irritability. These symptoms prove difficult for many to overcome as caffeine is addictive.

I find that many of my clients need to improve their nutrition and use strategies to improve their energy first before they can stop coffee. During the process of supporting their adrenal glands and improving the food they eat, they find that they no longer use coffee to keep them going and then they can easily give up coffee or use it as a social beverage with friends rather than a necessity for energy.

5. **Start your day with apple cider vinegar or lemon juice.** Two tablespoons of apple cider vinegar or lemon juice mixed in a small amount of water first thing during the day helps overall health. Much of the benefits of apple cider vinegar and lemon juice are anecdotal, which means that the benefits are based upon personal experience, rather than scientific trials. In any case, I recommend starting your day off with a small amount, and many of my clients feel better in many ways just after a few weeks of daily doses.

The bitter taste on the tongue from the apple cider vinegar or lemon juice is known to help stimulate liver detoxification pathways. Compounds from the apple cider vinegar are also found in the energy production pathway of the body, called the Krebs cycle. Ayurvedic medicine has used warm lemon juice for centuries as part of their liver detoxification regime.

6. **Make fruits, salad and vegetables the hero of your plate**. Many fruits, salad and vegetables contain phytochemicals and other nutrients that support your liver function. Foods such as beetroot, spinach leaves, rocket lettuce, cauliflower, broccoli, brussels sprouts, cabbage, kale, onions, garlic, ginger, turmeric, rosemary, coriander, parsley, berries, rockmelon, pawpaw and lemon, have a variety of phytochemicals that promote and support liver function. For instance, broccoli contains a chemical compound called sulforaphane that has been shown to promote liver detoxification pathways, stimulate genes and can help prevent some cancers.

   Consuming a variety of fresh fruits and vegetables daily will help support your health and well-being without needing a university degree to decipher the food compounds. Ensure you have a variety of colours when choosing your fruits and vegetables, and use predominantly seasonal produce to provide these nutrients.

7. **Keep your body hydrated.** As 80% of the body's composition is made of water, many of the cells require water to participate in the cellular chemical reactions and move chemicals in to or out of the cells. Without adequate hydration many cellular processes cannot proceed properly. You feel tired and foggy in thought when you are dehydrated.

The liver cannot process toxin removal without good hydration. Water is the medium that the liver uses to flush out the toxins that have been metabolised. Without adequate hydration, the bowels cannot eliminate faecal matter containing the toxins.

Hydration can come from filtered water, coconut water with no added sugar, and non-caffeinated herbal teas. Many types of fruits are high in water content and can add to your hydration level. Ensure that you are properly hydrated to help the liver undertake its detoxification processes. Chapter 3 will look further into water intake and your requirements.

8. **Remember to take a break and relax.** Adequate rest and relaxation are a necessity to help an overwhelmed liver. Constant stress creates stress hormones such as cortisol and adrenaline. If you're constantly stressed and always rushing, your liver must continually break down these stress hormones, placing it under extra load. Ensuring that you take a break to relax will help stop the adrenals from overproducing these stress hormones. Using fun, relaxing activities such as meditation, going for a walk, listening to good music or watching a comedy television show can do just that.

9. **Get good, refreshing sleep.** As you sleep during the night, your liver continues to perform detoxification actions, so if you're waking up between one and three o'clock in the middle of the night, that could be a sign that your liver is struggling. Getting good quality, refreshing sleep, going to bed the same time every night and waking up the same time every day will help your liver carry out its detoxification functions during the night. I address sleep and how to ensure a good sleep in Chapter 9.

10. **Opt for natural and organic products for your daily care.** What chemicals do you apply to your body on a daily basis? The personal care products we use can increase the number of chemicals the liver needs to process to an estimated 100,000 chemicals. There are many hidden chemicals in our skincare products and perfumes as companies do not necessarily list all the ingredients on their product labels, so you may not know how many chemicals are directly absorbed into your bloodstream as you apply them on to your skin each day. The liver has to filter and metabolise these chemicals, many of which have been shown to be toxic, nerve irritants, disruptive to our hormones and cancer-causing.

    The best thing you can do is to source truly organic products from reputable brands. Don't use products that have the word 'fragrance', 'perfume' or '*parfum*' as these words can hide over 3,000 chemicals without needing to list them all out.

    This is an area that you may find overwhelming as it can involve changing all the products you currently use on your skin, in your hair, in your mouth, as well as the cleaning products you use for your home. Instead of throwing your hands up in the air and say it is too hard, start by changing one product at a time as they run out, or attend one of the workshops I run on how to remove these chemicals from your daily life. Visit my website *www.teressatodd.com* to find out more about my workshops on this subject.

11. **Use herbs to cleanse and detoxify your liver.** Herbs have been shown to help support liver function and stimulate the regeneration of the liver. The herbs that I use in my clinic to help support liver function include St Mary's Thistle, Schisandra, Oregon Grape, Globe Artichoke, Fringe Tree and Turmeric.

Use these herbs in a lower dose over a couple of months to support the liver, as opposed to an intense, quick liver detoxification programme which can overwhelm you, especially when you are already struggling to keep up with your daily load. Fast detox programmes can cause you to feel more tired and unable to function for up to a week. This is fine if you are able to take the week off work, family duties and other roles.

If you need to maintain your energy levels for daily functioning, consider taking the gradual and slower route over a couple of months. My clients comment that they feel better only after four weeks of liver support formula.

As many liver herbs have interactions with other medications, it is best to seek advice from a qualified herbalist to ensure you have the correct liver support herbs for your situation.

Making changes in your life to help ease the burden on your liver will take time, but these changes will help to improve your energy, reduce fogginess of the mind, help your concentration, reduce anxiety and irritability, help you lose unwanted fat, and contribute to your ability to handle the everyday stresses that occur as a mum.

Change always comes hand in hand with trepidation, so start small. Change your eating structure to include the liver-enhancing foods, stop alcohol for four weeks and increase your fluid intake. Once you start to feel better with these changes then proceed to include the other changes in your daily life over the next month. Creating change slowly will help create a positive habit rather than a fad that you'll grow sick of.

3. Clarify Your Kidneys

'When you take the time to cleanse your physical body of accumulated stress and toxicity, you are rewarded with increased vitality and optimal health.'

– Debbie Ford

The next filter, the kidneys, are often neglected, but are just as vitally linked to your fatigue and energy.

There's two of them, sitting sit just underneath the lowest rib in your back. The kidneys filter the blood before going back to the heart, expelling water-soluble toxins and eliminating waste from the blood through the urine as it passes through. Kidneys play a role in the regulation of blood pH, maintenance of the fluid balance and control of the mineral balance – minerals known as electrolytes which are involved in energy production – of your body.

The main action of the kidney that relates to fatigue, energy and frazzled feelings is the ability of the kidney to remove the waste products from our bodies. These waste products can come from protein metabolism, by-products of bile from the liver, ammonia, drugs, food additives, excess hormones, etc. All of these need to be eliminated from the body to maintain a healthy function for daily life. So, it's not just about a matter of drinking water and hoping the kidneys will do their job.

Similar to the liver, the kidneys have several jobs or roles to play in the body. Not only do they excrete toxins but are also involved in creating hormones to direct the production of red blood cells from the bone marrow. The red blood cells act as a vehicle carrying oxygen and nutrients around the body. The hormones produced by the kidneys support your bone health, conversion of vitamin D to its active form, and blood pressure regulation.

Stress tends to put strain on the kidneys because of the increase in blood pressure during stressful periods. The blood pressure is increased to allow the muscles and heart to get more oxygen from the blood. Think about the scenario that you were being chased by a tiger, you would need extra blood pumping to the muscles so that you could run away. In our current time of stress – not being due to tigers, but instead due to deadlines, family pressures, financial issues and emotional strains – we still increase our blood pressure as a defence mechanism for the duration of the stressful event.

In western medicine we look at the kidney as an organ that has the specific jobs mentioned above, however in traditional Chinese medicine, the kidney is referred to as an organ-meridian system that stores *Qi* (pronounced 'chi'). It is the source of our inherited energy and has a relationship to the adrenals – which sit just above the kidneys. Kidney energy can gradually be depleted throughout our life and is particularly affected by overworking, insufficient fluid intake, multiple pregnancies (especially close together), chronic illness and stress. Does this sound familiar to a working mum in our current time?

To see if your kidneys are overburdened, tick the symptoms that relate to you:

- ❏ Suffer from regular headaches
- ❏ General fatigue
- ❏ Loss of appetite
- ❏ Itchy, dry skin
- ❏ Unexplained nausea
- ❏ Unintentional weight loss
- ❏ Pain in mid to lower back region
- ❏ Puffiness around eyes
- ❏ Trouble sleeping or insomnia
- ❏ Inability to concentrate
- ❏ Muscle cramps
- ❏ Fluid retention in hands, feet and ankles
- ❏ Strong smelling urine
- ❏ Dark coloured urine
- ❏ Frequent urination
- ❏ Sensation of coldness in the back
- ❏ Weakness of legs
- ❏ Night sweats

If you have ticked six or more boxes, it's time to look at ways to ease the burden and support your kidney's function as a filter.

Give Your Kidneys a Helping Hand

Water

The number one thing you can do to support your kidneys is hydration. Fluids are essential to filtering toxins and waste products.

Water is a substance that is vital to life. All living organisms need water to survive. Your body is made up of about 80% water. That is a lot of water in one body. You have to keep replenishing that water daily to maintain a healthy functioning of the body. An adult can survive weeks without food but only a few days without water. If a person loses more than 10% of their body water, they will slip into a coma and die.

Many clients say to me that they just don't feel thirsty. Thirst can come from a physiological need for water due to cellular changes in the body or it can be a natural response. I recommend that you drink water regularly throughout the whole day as thirst is not a reliable indicator for dehydration or optimal kidney function. If you find that you hardly feel thirsty throughout the day, set an alarm on your phone to remind you each hour to drink water.

I have encountered clients that say they don't like the taste of water. I recommend that you add an herbal tea flavour such as mint or rosehips, add pieces of fruit such as watermelon, strawberries or limes, or try adding mint leaves from your garden to your water. Find a flavour that you like and add that to start with. You will find that eventually you may not need the flavour as your body filters become more efficient.

Another question that I often get asked is how much a person should drink daily. The trick is to drink enough fluid to help optimise the kidneys without overloading them with excess fluid. An average woman should consume about 1.5 to 2 litres of filtered water a day. The average male is about 2.5 litres of filtered water a day.

If you want to calculate your required water intake, the following is a good guide:

Bodyweight in kilograms x 0.033 = how many litres of fluid per day

For example: a 60 kg person x 0.033 = 1.98 litres of water per day

If you are reading this and thinking, 'How am I going to drink 2 litres of water when I already struggle to drink one small glass', then start by aiming for 750 ml a day and then build up to 2 litres over the next one to two weeks. Use your phone alarm to remind yourself to drink a cup each hour. As you do this consistently, you will find that you want to drink more each day as you evidently feel better as a result of increased water intake.

Symptoms of mild dehydration include tiredness, confusion, irritability, dizziness, dry skin, headaches, muscle cramps, blurry vision and weakness. Many of my clients who come in with regular headaches and fatigue feel better after increasing their fluid intake.

Diuretic Drinks

Reduce drinks such as coffee, tea, caffeinated soft drinks and alcohol. These drinks have a diuretic action which encourages the kidneys to excrete more urine. This can place an extra burden on the kidneys and can contribute to dehydration. There is a temptation to opt for a soft drink, cordial, electrolyte drink or energy drink when you are thirsty, when in fact, they can actually contribute to your dehydration. Remember I said that water helps to remove toxins and wastes from the body; diuretic beverages can contain chemicals that require the body to use water to help remove them, therefore you would be worse off as far as hydration is concerned.

Urine Colour Is the Key

Use urine as an indicator of hydration and toxicity. If you are adequately hydrated you would urinate several times per day, and the urine would be light in colour. When dehydration or high toxicity occur, urine becomes dark yellow and can have a strong odour. Use the 'wee test' to determine your hydration levels. Aim for pale straw coloured urine without a strong odour. If you are taking vitamin B supplements or a multivitamin then the urine will become bright yellow as a consequence of the metabolism of the vitamin B, so factor this into your wee test process. As you drink water throughout the day the bright yellow colour should subside.

Keep in mind that the water you drink needs to be pure. Drink water without additives and use a filtration device – either one attached to your sink or a separate filter canister. These devices can help remove chemicals such as chlorine, lead, organic pesticides and other nasties from your water. Filtration devices range in price, reliable and inexpensive options can easily be purchased from reputable health food shops or online.

Salty and Processed Foods

Reducing your consumption of table salt or food high in salt will benefit your kidney health in the long run. Although sodium from table salt is important for the health of the kidneys and helps to pull the water from the blood into the kidney for filtration, it needs to be balanced with potassium. Sodium and potassium are electrolytes of the body that are needed for cellular fluid balance and good heart function. When your diet is too high in sodium the kidney function is reduced and less water is being filtered. High sodium consumption is linked to high blood pressure and this places an extra demand on the kidneys. On the other hand, low potassium can lead to fatigue, weakness, muscle cramps, heart palpitations and tingling sensations.

The majority of processed foods are high in sodium, and for the health of your kidneys I recommend reducing processed foods and the addition of table salt in your meals. Use Celtic sea salt instead as it has a myriad of minerals to maintain the electrolyte balance of the body without adding further demands to your kidney system.

When clients are having difficulties with fluid retention and need to support the kidney function I recommend that they add celery, banana, cucumber, apricots, parsley, goji berries, lemons, asparagus and beetroot to their diet. Maybe enjoy a glass of juice each day that contains carrot, apple, celery, beetroot, ginger and parsley; snack on goji berries and nuts as your afternoon snack, or include goji berries in a your homemade muesli bar. For added support, I use herbs such as Rehmannia, Horsetail, Dandelion Leaf, Goldenrod,

Nettle and Cleavers. As with all herbs it is best to have a qualified herbalist's advice to select the correct herbs for your health as many of these herbs can interact with other medications.

Action Time

Take care of your kidneys by ensuring adequate hydration, reducing salt and diuretic drinks – this will help you feel livelier and more energised throughout the day. Symptoms of dehydration alone will contribute to your fatigue and foggy thought, so do yourself a favour and fill up on your filtered water today. Check your urine to guide you on how much water you require.

4. Power Up Your Adrenals and Thyroid

'Stress is not what happens to us. It's our response TO what happens. And RESPONSE is something we can choose.'

– Maureen Killoran

When it comes to feeling energised, the function of the adrenals and the thyroid is important. Understanding how these glands can influence your energy production will help you to take control and rid yourself of fatigue. When your adrenals and thyroid are functioning optimally, you will be able to deal with your stress easier, you will regain your motivation and drive, you will reduce your need for cat naps and not have to push your tired self through the day.

You can restore that long-term energy and stamina once you start taking care of your thyroid and adrenals.

The thyroid and the adrenals are two endocrine organs that play a role in regulating your get-up-and-go energy. When these two organ systems are not working efficiently, you can be left feeling tired, fatigued and run-down. Some of the symptoms that can occur with sub-optimal functioning can include fatigue, foggy thought, trouble concentrating, lack of motivation, anxiety, weight gain, inability to cope with stressful events, and the inability to multitask.

As a mum, when you are running around doing all the jobs and the roles that many women do, you tend to burn the candle at both ends and the body creates stress hormones to keep you going. In my clinic I find that many women are doing everything they can for their family, job, partner, friends, and oftentimes there's no energy or time set aside for themselves, they just don't stop and they constantly push themselves day in and day out. This perpetual energy needs to be generated from somewhere and these two organ systems need to keep producing hormones to make this energy.

The body can keep making the necessary energy for a period of time, but when it runs out you become fatigued. To replenish your energy tank, you must address the thyroid and the adrenals that have been keeping you going for all this time. Firstly, let's have a look at the all too common reason that's preventing your thyroid and adrenals from functioning at their optimal levels – stress.

What Is Stress?

When you hear the word 'stress', what do you think of? Do you think deadlines at work or running late for an appointment? Perhaps you think about the traffic jam on the way to pick up the children or all the meal prep that needs to be done for the week.

The one definition of stress in the dictionary is 'a state of mental or emotional strain resulting from adverse or demanding circumstances.' The medical term for stress implies that it is a factor that causes a physical or mental reaction.

Stress can come in different forms. A physical form of stress could be an injury, chronic pain or a chronic illness. Physical stress can also include toxins that you are exposed to such as environmental toxins or chemicals from your workplace. Another form of stress could come from mental factors, such as thinking about the list of things you need to do when you get home, worrying about your children, financial pressure, depression, or the demands of your workload. Mentally we can just worry about everything or have recurring negative thoughts going around in our head. I have clients come in and say, 'I just worry about everything. My family says I will always find something to worry about.'

Stress can also include emotional triggers, such as relationship problems, social issues, or our own emotional demands that we place on ourselves as women and mums.

All these factors will have an impact on you and cause your body to make a physical response that comes from the adrenal glands.

What Are the Adrenal Glands?

They are the two glands that sit on top of the kidneys and produce a hormone called adrenaline. This hormone increases the blood circulation to our muscles, increases our heart rate, blood pressure and respiration rate. Adrenaline mobilises any stored glucose in our muscles so that we have a fuel source in readiness to run away from or fight our threat.

Imagine again the tiger that was chasing you, your adrenal glands will produce adrenaline, which mobilises the fuel stored in your body. This fuel helps power your muscles in order to work harder – you'll run faster than you have ever ran before! The fuel also helps you breathe more, this will transport more oxygen to your muscles – further powering your muscles and enabling you to run faster.

In this scenario, the threat of the tiger chasing after you would usually be of short duration and over in a matter of minutes or hours. The threats that exist in this modern time are threats that can last for days, weeks, months, or in some cases, even years at a time.

When a threat remains for a long period of time, the adrenal glands will then produce another hormone called cortisol – a long-term chronic stress hormone. Cortisol is produced when adrenaline levels have been high for too long. In tribal or more primitive times, high cortisol would have been produced in times of drought, famine or major floods.

In the current time of the modern woman, cortisol is produced as a result of long-term stresses such as financial concerns, relationship issues, family demands, work demands, or a combination of all of them which overwhelms the body.

How Does High Cortisol Affect Your Body?

When the stresses continue over a prolonged period of time and cortisol is produced constantly, it can have detrimental effects to our bodies. Initially, the cortisol will make you feel energised and able to cope. Over time the high cortisol and added nutritional demand that goes with it will start to make you feel tired. The adrenals start to fatigue, you put on weight for no apparent reason, you feel tired or exhausted, and you can't think straight.

Does any of this sound familiar?

With high cortisol levels, you begin to store more fat in your body, especially around the waist and the upper arms. If you tend to put on weight around the belly, getting that muffin top, or fat on the back of the arms (aka tuckshop arms), it could be due to the high cortisol level in your body. The thyroid is affected by the high cortisol, and this in turn slows down your body's metabolism. You may find that your muscle mass is reducing as your body breaks down muscles as a fuel source. When the muscle mass reduces, the metabolism further slows down and compounds the weight gain.

Complete the following questionnaire to see if you could be fatigued due to your adrenals.

Tick the symptoms that relate to you:

- ❏ Struggle to wake up in the morning; or feel unrefreshed after sleep
- ❏ Feel tired in the morning, need a coffee or stimulant to 'wake up' and then feel tired again around 2 to 5 pm
- ❏ Struggle to fall asleep at night even though you feel tired
- ❏ Feel extremely tired in the evenings but get a 'second wind' after 10 pm
- ❏ Gained weight recently, especially around your middle
- ❏ Need to snack regularly to keep from feeling tired and shaky
- ❏ Suffer recurrent infections
- ❏ Feel shaky, cranky or fatigued if you skip meals
- ❏ Have brain fog or poor memory
- ❏ Have trouble concentrating
- ❏ Feel anxious often
- ❏ Difficulty dealing with stress or deadlines
- ❏ Feel dizziness, especially upon standing
- ❏ Find it hard to relax or feeling tense all the time

- ❏ Unable to cope with small added pressures or feel overwhelmed easily
- ❏ Noticed loss of muscle tone recently even though there are no changes in exercise routine
- ❏ Suffer premenstrual syndrome symptoms such as heavy bleeding, mood changes, or fatigue with menstrual cycle
- ❏ Have low libido

Add up the number of boxes you ticked.

If you scored 8 or more, you may be suffering from adrenal fatigue.

Adrenal fatigue is a term used in natural medicine to describe a group of symptoms – such as fatigue, sleep issues, digestive issues and body aches – that occur when the adrenal glands function below their optimal level. Another term used instead of adrenal fatigue is adrenal insufficiency whereby the adrenal glands are unable to produce enough hormones needed to keep up with the demands of the continual stress response.

The best test for determining your cortisol levels and therefore adrenal function is the 24-hour salivary cortisol test. This test needs to be done through a qualified health practitioner and can help detect your daily cortisol cycle. From this you will be able to determine your adrenal function in relation to cortisol production.

Cortisol is normally highest in the morning, which stimulates you to wake up. If cortisol is low in the morning you will find it hard to wake up and get going – you wake up feeling tired and unrefreshed. The evening is when cortisol should be at its lowest. This enables you to go to sleep. If your cortisol is high in the evening you won't be able to get good quality sleep. 24-hour salivary cortisol testing will reveal how your cortisol is fluctuating during the day.

Tips for Supporting the Adrenals

Nutritional support of the adrenals is important to combat adrenal fatigue. The adrenals need key nutrients to help with its function.

Load your diet with lots of vitamin C-based foods. This includes oranges, lemons, strawberries, cherries, papayas, kiwifruit, capsicums, melons, brussels sprouts, dark leafy veggies, broccoli, cauliflower and tomato.

All the B group vitamins are important to help support the adrenals, especially vitamin B5, vitamin B6 and vitamin B12. Food sources of these B vitamins include avocados, bananas, spinach, green beans, broccoli, eggplant, mushrooms, sunflower seeds, eggs, salmon, beef, lamb and chicken. Zinc is also an important mineral that helps maintain optimal adrenal functioning. Food sources for zinc include lean meat, shellfish, pepitas, hemp seeds, nuts, dairy products and eggs.

In previous chapters, I have spoken about caffeine and sugar interfering with the functions of the filters. The same applies here. They rob the adrenals of vital nutrients and place a higher demand upon the production of the adrenal hormones. Avoid these to help restore your adrenal function and your energy.

Become aware of the stresses that are present in your daily life. Some of these stresses can be eliminated. Some stresses may be out of your control, but if you become aware of the stresses and you take steps to change how you respond to them, you will significantly reduce the taxing effect stress has on your adrenals. Look at which tigers are chasing you and give some of them the flick. In effect, the adrenals will not be overburdened with the constant production of those stress hormones. Take some time to relax and recharge so that your adrenals glands can do the same. Look at Chapter 10, Recharge ME, for help around this.

There are several herbs that can be used as adrenal tonics that help support the function of the adrenals. In my clinic I use herbs such as Rhodiola, Liquorice, Siberian Ginseng, Withania and Rehmannia as part of a treatment programme to help women restore their adrenal balance and energy. We take a closer look at these nutrition-packed herbs in Chapter 8, Magic Herbs and Nutrients.

The Thyroid and Your Fatigue

The adrenals don't work alone when helping a stressed-out woman cope in today's high-pressure times.

The thyroid is another organ that conveys messages for the body's energy production. The thyroid is a gland that sits in the front of your neck, just above your collar bones. The role of the thyroid is to create thyroid hormones that influence the metabolism of the food you eat. It also influences your heart rate, blood pressure, digestion, muscle strength, body temperature, sex hormones and breathing rate.

There is a communication highway between the thyroid, liver, adrenals and the brain; if a miscommunication occurs between any of them or if one organ system is weakened from chronic stress, your energy production will be affected. When the body is experiencing stressful events, the thyroid function increases, this results in an increased need for nutrients such as tyrosine, selenium, iron and iodine.

Nutritional imbalances and toxins deplete the thyroid and its function. This has a flow-on effect to the rest of your body, leaving you feeling tired and fatigued, with low libido, foggy thought, weight gain and sensitivity to cold temperatures.

The thyroid hormone cascade starts with the hypothalamus (in the brain), it signals the pituitary gland to make thyroid-stimulating hormone (TSH) and this hormone then signals the thyroid to make thyroxin (T4). This hormone is not active and must be activated to create a response in the body of boosting metabolism and burning body fat for energy. The activated thyroid hormone is called tri-iodothyronine (T3).

Thyroid dysfunction can occur in up to 10% of women in their first year after pregnancy. It can resolve itself naturally, but in some cases it can remain and cause other diseases if left untreated.

Thyroid function can also be affected by autoimmune conditions. Grave's disease and Hashimoto's thyroiditis are increasing in prevalence in my clinic. Hashimoto's thyroiditis is an autoimmune condition of the thyroid where the thyroid becomes underactive; symptoms of fatigue, weight gain, foggy thought, slow thought, anxiety and constipation are common. On the other hand, Grave's disease is at the other end of the autoimmune spectrum where the thyroid is overactive and producing too much thyroid hormones; symptoms include weight loss, tremors, anxiety, bulging eyes and fast talking. I find that many clients have autoimmune thyroid conditions but are unaware of it and testing is needed to identify it.

As part of the investigation process for fatigue, I recommend that you test your thyroid hormones and antibodies. Get a full thyroid function blood test performed to check your thyroid's levels of anti-thyroid peroxidase antibodies (anti-TPO), anti-thyroglobulin antibodies (anti-TG), thyroid stimulating hormone (TSH), inactive thyroid hormone T4 and active thyroid hormone T3.

Keep in mind that most routine thyroid tests will only show the results for TSH levels. The routine laboratory tests for TSH alone are not sensitive enough to pick up many of the thyroid conditions. In Australia, many doctors have their hands tied when requests are made by patients to get precise thyroid tests that shows results beyond TSH levels, especially when the initial test has shown results in the normal range.

In my clinic I have seen many test results show the TSH level within the normal range in the pathology test, but there were still other antibodies present or the conversion of the thyroid hormones was not adequate. It's good to have a thorough look at all the parameters of the thyroid.

If you suspect that there is a thyroid imbalance causing your fatigue and other symptoms, then look for an experienced health practitioner that can help you with the testing and interpretation of the results.

For instance, during my first pregnancy, my TSH level was 3.8 – within the normal range for the pathology blood tests. A few months after my daughter was born I discovered that I had

Hashimoto's thyroiditis, it wasn't identified as part of the routine pathology testing as it was within the normal range. Hence, it is always best to have a thorough look at the different parameters and not just rely on one parameter.

Take the following questionnaire to determine whether your thyroid could be related to your fatigue and other symptoms. Tick the symptoms that relate to you:

- ❑ Ongoing fatigue
- ❑ Put on weight easily
- ❑ Flaky or dry skin
- ❑ Dry, brittle hair and/or nails
- ❑ Excessive hair falling out
- ❑ Puffy hands and feet
- ❑ Weak muscles and/or weak limbs
- ❑ Slow reflexes
- ❑ Constipation or sluggish bowel
- ❑ Low mood
- ❑ Irritability
- ❑ Depression
- ❑ Poor memory
- ❑ Low libido
- ❑ Heavy periods
- ❑ More frequent periods
- ❑ Feel cold easily

Add up the number of boxes you have ticked.

If you scored 8 or more, you may have a thyroid imbalance which can be contributing to your fatigue symptoms.

Tips for Supporting the Thyroid

If your thyroid function is low, it is best to investigate and find out the cause, if it is purely nutrition-related or if it is due to an autoimmune condition. In any case, you must ensure your digestive system is functioning optimally and that your diet contains the nutrients needed for thyroid hormone conversion.

Nutritional deficiencies would need to be addressed in order to support a healthy thyroid. The nutrients that are important for the thyroid include selenium, iodine, tyrosine and iron.

Selenium is a mineral that is important not only for your thyroid, but also aids in liver detoxification and acts as an antioxidant nutrient helping to prevent many cancers. Soils in Australia are deficient in selenium, hence much of the food produced here are deficient in it. A good reliable source for selenium is brazil nut. One to two handfuls per day can help replete your levels.

Iodine is a mineral that is important for thyroid and mental functioning. Seafoods, seaweeds and sea salt are good sources of iodine. Even though Australia is surrounded by the sea, I find that many clients just don't eat enough seafoods and seaweeds to give them adequate iodine. Using Celtic sea salt on meals will help. In the 1970s and 1980s iodised table salt was widely used, giving a source of iodine. Today's studies have shown that table salt is not good for our health, so other forms of iodine need to be sourced.

Accurate iodine testing should be done before supplementing with this mineral, as too much iodine has dire health consequences. Testing can be done through a 24-hour urine test requested through your health practitioner.

Tyrosine is an amino acid that is produced in the body from phenylalanine and can also be found in chicken, turkey, fish, milk, yogurt, dairy products, eggs, peanuts, almonds, pumpkin seeds, sesame seeds, soy products, lima beans, avocados and bananas. Tyrosine is needed for the manufacturing of thyroid hormones. If you are depleted in tyrosine, you may have issues in making your thyroid hormones. Tyrosine is also used in other areas of the body including the production of the brain chemicals dopamine and norepinephrine. These brain chemicals help elevate your mood and help with relaxation.

If the thyroid is imbalanced, then investigate your sex hormone balance of estrogen as too much estrogen can have a negative impact on the thyroid. The sex hormones, estrogen and progesterone, can be tested through the blood or saliva. The full effects of these hormones are discussed in the next chapter.

Keep in mind that the thyroid's functioning also relies on the liver. Ensure that the liver is functioning to its full potential as the thyroid is sensitive to toxins. Use the techniques that have already been addressed in Chapter 2.

Action Time

Supporting the thyroid and the adrenals is vitally important to restoring your vibrant energy levels. By looking at the role of both these organs and their role in your stress response, you can make positive changes to regain your energy.

Look to assessing your thyroid and adrenal functions through testing provided by a qualified health practitioner. Replenishing the adrenals and the thyroid takes time. Allow the nutrients to be absorbed into the body and to run its healing processes in order to get those organ systems back into balance again. Please don't expect them to rebalance themselves overnight. Supplementation using a good quality supplement that supports the thyroid and adrenals can help fast track the healing process, but your food choices are the way to go for long-term health. Work with a qualified health professional to help you on your journey and track your progress.

5. Hormone Chaos

'When your hormones are out of balance, you will find it harder to balance your mood, energy and stress response.'

– Teressa Todd

Women have a myriad of hormones in their bodies that intricately interact with each other. A hormone is a chemical substance that is produced by specific cells of the body to control and regulate the activity of other cells or organs. There are many types of hormones, including the thyroid hormones and adrenal hormones – which we looked at in the previous chapters – there's also the sleep hormones and growth hormones, as well as the sex hormones – which we will look at now. The sex hormones include estrogen, progesterone and testosterone.

Estrogen and progesterone are involved with the regulation of the menstrual cycle and fertility, but they also contribute to your moods (sanity), energy, inflammation, weight, relaxation, drive and motivation. Women have smaller quantities of testosterone compared to men, and it needs to be in balance with estrogen and progesterone. Testosterone plays a role in libido, drive and energy.

The sex hormones create and regulate the menstrual cycle. The way you can tell if there is an imbalance in your menstrual cycle is to look at the symptoms of premenstrual syndrome, the flow and length of your period, and conditions such as polycystic ovarian syndrome (PCOS), fibroids and endometriosis. Any changes or symptoms can indicate that your cycle is not balanced and needs attention.

The prevalence of hormone-related conditions are increasing in my clinic. Is this due to the increased awareness and testing for hormonal conditions, or is the current modern era contributing to the increase in hormonal imbalances in women in general? In my opinion it is more likely to be the latter. There are many lifestyle conditions that influence our delicate hormonal balance, including stress, excess exercise, rapid weight loss, irregular sleep, poor nutrition and diet, illness and poor liver function.

It seems that the lifestyle of the modern era for women has a huge impact on hormonal imbalance. The superwoman who is always on the go, has many roles to perform each day and doesn't get adequate sleep is at risk of hormonal imbalance. Add those to the constant exposure to environmental chemicals that disrupt or mimic our hormones. Despite all the downside, there are ways to get around them, and with the right actions you can overcome the chaos with your hormones.

A Hormone Overview

The hormonal cycle is exactly that, a cycle of various hormones throughout the month. Each part of the cycle has a purpose and triggers the next part of the cycle to flow on. Any imbalance to this will change the flow-on effect through the rest of the cycle.

The pituitary gland in the brain produces hormones called luteinising hormone (LH) and follicle stimulating hormone (FSH). These two hormones are involved in stimulating the ovary to produce estrogen and then progesterone.

During the first half of the cycle (around fourteen days), the ovary is stimulated to produce estrogen. This stimulates the uterine lining – or endometrium – to develop in readiness for egg implantation and pregnancy. A small amount of progesterone is produced from the adrenal glands in the first half of the cycle. As estrogen increases, the egg – or ovum – develops and matures and is released at ovulation. Once released, the egg travels to the uterus ready for implantation. The capsule that is left behind in the ovary after the egg is released is called the corpus luteum, and this produces progesterone during the second half of the menstrual cycle (around the last fourteen days). During this stage, estrogen decreases initially and is then sustained at the lowered amount.

The hypothalamus in the brain detects all these activities and levels in the blood, and then sends feedbacks to the pituitary gland. If levels are not in the correct balance, the pituitary gland will try to correct them through the FSH and LH production. This is known as the feedback loop and it's how the body tries to maintain consistency.

Progesterone, testosterone and estrogen are all produced from cholesterol, as is your stress hormone, cortisol. If one of these hormone pathways are imbalanced, it has a flow-on effect on the other hormonal pathways. From this, you can see that if you are stressed and producing lots of cortisol it can steal the cholesterol from another pathway such as the one needed to make progesterone. Hormonal imbalance inevitably follows.

What Role Does Estrogen Have?

Estrogen is produced mainly in the ovaries. It can also be produced – in much smaller quantities – in the liver, pancreas, adrenals, adipose tissue and breast.

There are three main types of estrogen – estradiol, estrone, and estriol. Estradiol is the active form of estrogen that is produced from the ovaries. Estrone and estriol are weaker in action. Estrone is produced by the fat and muscle and can be converted into the stronger acting estradiol. Estriol is mainly produced during pregnancy.

The action of estrogen is to stimulate growth of the endometrium, promote bone density, and maintain the structure of the skin and blood vessels. Estrogen also has a function in heart health, aids memory and stimulates fat around the abdomen, hips and breasts.

Due to the stimulation of growth, estrogen needs to be broken down once it has served its purpose. If not broken down correctly, they can cause fibroids, endometriosis and some cancers. Estrogen is broken down in the liver to less active forms and excreted into the bile to be eliminated through the intestines. Some estrogens are recycled (remade) in the intestines by the beneficial intestinal bacteria and sent back into circulation.

As I stated at the beginning, hormones are kept at a delicate balance in order to maintain healthy body functions. Since all the hormones act together, the healthy levels of hormones are measured in relation to each other. For instance, progesterone deficiency occurs when progesterone is lower than estrogen and testosterone. Estrogen excess occurs when estrogen is higher than progesterone.

Low estrogen can trigger symptoms such as hot sweats, poor fertility, low libido, irregular periods or no periods, excess dryness of vaginal area which can cause painful sexual intercourse, low bone density, mood swings, depression and increased urinary tract infections.

Menopausal symptoms often occur due to the low estrogen or estrogen deficiency. Premenopausal women can have low estrogen due to too much estrogen being broken down or too little recycled in the intestinal tract.

Tips to Help Correct Low Estrogen Levels

1. Decrease the fibre supplements in your diet. Instead, opt to take natural fibres found in fruits and vegetables which will help increase the bacteria in the intestines that recycle estrogen. Beware that antibiotics will alter the intestinal microbial load and influence their ability to recycle estrogen.

2. Increase your vitamin A and beta-carotene intake, these are found in butter, cod liver oil, carrots, tomatoes, rockmelon, apricots, mangoes, peaches, pumpkin and sweet potato.

3. Avoid smoking as it will significantly lower your estrogen levels.

4. Excessive exercise reduces your estrogen levels compared to testosterone. While exercise is great, keep it to a moderate level and don't overdo it. A good guideline is thirty to forty-five minutes, five times per week, with a combination of cardio and resistance exercise. Allow yourself sufficient rest between exercise.

5. Herbs that may help with estrogen deficiency include Wild Yam, Liquorice and Dong Quai. Before using herbs, get qualified herbal advice and look at testing to determine your estrogen level.

High estrogen or estrogen dominance does not necessarily mean the ovaries produce too much estrogen, it could also be caused by the lack of adequate breakdown of the circulating estrogen, or the overexposure to environmental estrogens called xenoestrogens.

Symptoms include heavy period, longer than usual periods, headaches and migraines, depression, mood swings, brain fog, insomnia, anxiety, breast tenderness, fatigue, low libido, unexplained weight gain and fibrocystic breasts.

Tips to Help Correct High Estrogen Dominance

1. Reduce your refined carbohydrates such as white bread, white rice, processed sugars and confectionary.

2. Increase your fibre-containing foods such as wholegrains, quinoa, fruits and vegetables.

3. Reduced saturated fat such as fried foods, bakery products and red meat.

4. Include cultured foods such as yoghurts, sauerkraut, miso and kombucha. Start with a low amount and build up to larger quantities to help improve the intestinal bacteria levels that help balance estrogen.

5. Vitamin B6 helps stimulate the effects of estrogen. Foods high in vitamin B6 include organic chicken, silverbeet, eggplant, sunflower seeds and pistachio nuts.

6. Moderate level, low intensity exercises such as walking, swimming and cycling can help to reduce excessive estrogen – too much exercise will do the opposite.

7. Consume foods in the brassica family – broccoli, cauliflower, brussels sprouts – as they contain a phytochemical called indoles. These compounds help increase the rate of clearance of estrogen from the liver. Foods such as spinach, grapefruit, oranges, cherries and apples contains a compound called calcium d-glucarate. This compound helps the liver detoxify excessive estrogen and may help to reduce risks of hormone-sensitive cancers.

8. Relying solely on food to correct your hormone levels can sometimes be slow in helping balance the body. Indole-3-carbinol and calcium d-glucarate are fast-acting and available in supplemental forms. It is best to seek qualified naturopathic advice to see how these may help you.

9. Xenoestrogens can contribute to estrogen dominance. Xenoestrogens are compounds that mimic estrogen. These compounds can be found in foods, plants and the environment. Pesticides and soft plastics contain compounds such as nonylphenol and bisphenol-A. Perfumes and personal care products can contain thousands of compounds, including parabens, that can

mimic estrogen and are endocrine-disrupting. Single xenoestrogen compounds have little biological effect. The disruptive effects occur when there is a combination of these chemicals. Their effect can be multiplied by 1,000 times. Natural estrogens only circulate in your body for a short time – usually a few weeks – whereas xenoestrogens can circulate for years and accumulate during your lifetime.

10. There is not enough room in this book to go into all the xenoestrogens in your environment. If you want more information, visit my website *www.teressatodd.com* to download a checklist of the top-rated chemicals in your environment and good alternatives.

11. Limit any plastics that you use for storing food. Do not heat food in plastic. Use Pyrex to store and heat foods. Get BPA-free tinned food or avoid tinned food and canned drinks altogether.

12. Look at your personal care products. Get products that are organic and from reputable companies. There are reputable companies that ensure their products do not contain xenoestrogens. An app called *The Chemical Maze* can help you decipher the myriad of chemical names that are on consumer products and their effects.

13. The best way to reduce estrogen dominance is to optimise the liver detoxification pathways. Go back to Chapter 2 and look at how you can optimise your liver function.

Progesterone – The Happy Hormone

While estrogen causes tissues to grow, progesterone stimulates tissues to secrete. Under the influence of progesterone, the uterine lining of the uterus is stimulated to secrete and thicken in readiness for pregnancy, while the breasts are stimulated to secrete breast milk.

Progesterone helps to improve fat metabolism, improve bone density, elevate mood and reduce depression and anxiety, aid in clearer thinking, is a natural diuretic, and helps to prevent cancer in the breast and uterus.

Progesterone is a precursor to other hormones, such as cortisol, estrogen and testosterone. Due to this it can help maintain blood sugar levels, reduce inflammation and increase tolerance to stress.

Symptoms of low progesterone include low mood, depression, anxiety, unexplained weight gain and difficulty in losing weight, inability to conceive, fluid retention, fatigue and poor thyroid function.

Tips to Help Balance Progesterone Levels

1. Ensure you have optimal levels of magnesium which aids in the production of many hormones including progesterone. Magnesium can be found in almonds, cashews, macadamias, walnuts, brazil nuts, pine nuts, pecans, pistachios, cacao, eggs, figs, green leafy veggies, sunflower seeds, sesame seeds, apricots, apples, dates, prunes, bananas, spinach, parsley, shallots, legumes and coconut water.

2. Zinc is important for the manufacturing of all hormones. Food sources for zinc include pepitas, beans, animal meats, nuts, fish and other seafood.

3. Vitamin E can help in cases of progesterone deficiency. Foods high in vitamin E include sesame seeds, sunflower seeds, tahini, walnuts, almonds, macadamia and organic egg yolk.

4. Good fats help to balance progesterone. The fats from deep sea fish, evening primrose oil and avocado can help balance the prostaglandin hormones that are linked to progesterone.

5. Being overweight contributes to the imbalance between estrogen and progesterone. Aiming for a healthy weight will help balance out the progesterone–estrogen imbalance. Work with a qualified health professional to help during this process.

6. Avoid overeating and look to foods that are low in refined sugars. Keeping balanced blood sugar levels will in turn help balance your progesterone levels.

7. Stress is the major progesterone robber. Limit the stress in your life. While stress and the modern-day mother seem to come hand in hand, it doesn't have to be the norm. Using the techniques shown throughout this book will help to reduce your stress and the benefits will flow through to your hormones.

8. Ensure the thyroid is functioning optimally. Normal thyroid function helps to improve ovarian function and progesterone levels. In the previous chapter I addressed optimum thyroid function.

When progesterone is balanced you will feel more relaxed and calmer as progesterone is linked to a neurotransmitter, GABA. This brain chemical helps to counteract the effects of stress in the brain. It helps to induce relaxation, improves mood during mental tasks, help with multitasking ability and help promote good sleep.

What Are Androgens?

Androgens are responsible for the masculine effects on the body – male pattern hair, facial hair, deeper voice and decreased breast size.

Testosterone is one of the most well-known and most potent androgens. It is not just present in the male body. Females have lower levels than males and it needs to be kept in balance with estrogen and progesterone for optimum hormonal health. Testosterone is produced in the ovaries, fat and adrenals, and it is involved in libido, energy, brain function, muscle development and strength, and fat distribution.

Symptoms of high testosterone include menstrual irregularity or absence of periods, excess body hair and facial hair on chin and upper lip, acne, hair loss around hair line, change in body shape and loss of the female curve.

Polycystic ovarian syndrome (PCOS) is a condition related to high testosterone levels. Symptoms include excess facial hair, scalp hair loss, irregular periods, acne, unexplained weight gain, fertility issues, anxiety and depression. Blood tests and ultrasound can be done to check for PCOS, ask your doctor if you are concerned.

Tips to Help Balance Testosterone Levels

1. Eat regular meals to help balance blood sugar levels. If there is any blood sugar imbalance, look to use chromium and lipoic acid supplements to help. Herbs such as Gymnema, Nigella and cinnamon can help to regulate blood sugar levels.

2. Reduce your intake of refined carbohydrates like white sugar, white breads and pasta.

3. Exercise regularly, combining both resistance exercise and aerobic exercise. Aim for thirty to forty-five minutes of work out, five times per week.

4. Include in your diet essential fatty acids containing omega-3 fats such as flaxseed, flaxseed oil, hemp seeds, hemp seed oil, macadamia, almonds and walnuts.

5. Herbs such as Peony and Liquorice can help balance testosterone levels in females.

Testing Your Hormone Levels

The best method to assess your hormonal cycle is to get a cyclic salivary hormone test done. This test is done using a saliva sample collected on Day 3, 5, 8, 11, 12, 14, 16, 18, 20, 23 and 28. This will test your estrogen and progesterone levels eleven times over the duration of a month. The testosterone is only tested on Day 11. Doing a test like this will give you a pattern of your hormonal cycle and can help the health practitioner identify which part of your cycle needs support.

Single day blood tests are also available and can tell you the levels of your estrogen, progesterone and testosterone, but it can only give you a snapshot of part of your cycle. For a complete picture, opt for the cyclic salivary hormone test.

Action Plan

Find a qualified health practitioner experienced in hormones that will test your cyclic salivary hormones and help identify any hormonal imbalances. Once you have identified which hormone is causing your imbalance, you can take the above mentioned measures to correct the delicate hormone balance. This will set you on the path to regaining your health, energy, mood – and sanity!

6. Stealth Infections

'Living with chronic infection undermines your health and vitality. It is a silent invader that slowly wears away at your ability to live to your best.'

– Teressa Todd

Infections can rob you of your energy; they deplete your body nutritionally, cause your immune system and adrenals to burn out, leaving you feeling flattened and fatigued. Bacteria, viruses, parasites and other pathogens – the main culprits for infections – change how your body responds to its environment and rob you of the vital nutrients you need.

When an infective agent, or a pathogen, is not dealt with properly, it can become hidden or latent. As a result of this infectious agent, the body produces inflammatory chemicals called cytokines. These create overall inflammation in the body. When cytokines are produced long-term, fatigue always occurs as a result.

Identifying and correcting infections help provide an overall better energy, your immune system functions better, you have the stamina to do things consistently, you're better equipped to deal with everyday life; if a chronic, stealth or latent infection is allowed to linger, it will constantly undermine the body's immune system, leaving you weak and unable to defend yourself.

These infections can also lead to autoimmune conditions, chronic fatigue and many other degenerative diseases. As a clinical naturopath, I've seen many infections contribute to fatigue and ultimately lead to chronic diseases, leaving the person feeling weak and unable to enjoy life fully. Being a microbiologist as well, I studied microbes and infective agents in depth, and now use my expertise in both fields – microbiology and naturopathy – to help clients.

What Do Microorganisms Do?

The invention of the microscope in the 1800s opened the door to discovering bacteria and parasites, and later on viruses when the electron microscope was invented. Since then we have been able to identify many of the infective agents that can create fatigue and disease. In this chapter we will look at some of the pathogenic microorganisms that disrupt the regular function of your immune system and deplete your nutritional reserves, causing fatigue, disease and dysfunction.

Not all microorganisms are the bad guys. There are many microorganisms in and on the body that promote the health and functioning of a body. Consider the bacteria that exist in the intestines. There are many thousands of beneficial bacteria – also known as commensal organisms – in your intestines and they help support your immune system, metabolise toxins, assist neurotransmitter balance of the brain, and aid nutritional status. These commensal organisms – the good guys – can help support life and inhibit the pathogens – the bad guys.

Pathogens – The Bad Guys and Their Effects

What happens when an infective agent – aka pathogen or bad guy – enters the body? Firstly, the body responds by creating a fever to activate the immune system. This increases the number of white blood cells released to fight the infection and creates inflammatory chemicals to help defend against the pathogen. Depending on where the pathogen invades, there may be symptoms such as cough, mucus production, aches and pains, or diarrhoea. These are known as the acute reaction. This reaction has a finite length of time that it occurs and – depending on the strength of your immune system – can be very short lived. Generally, acute infections don't leave us feeling too depleted, most people bounce back within a few days.

Latent Infections

When an infection becomes latent or persistent, it can affect our energy levels. A latent infection occurs when the pathogens that invade our body produce an immediate reaction from the immune system, then it replicates and goes into hiding, lying dormant until the right conditions are ready for them to re-emerge and reinfect.

An example of this is the herpes virus that causes cold sores and shingles. Cold sores come and go at times when a person experiences late nights, sunburn or emotional stress. The papilloma virus that causes warts is another example of latent infection.

Epstein–Barr virus (EBV) is another latent virus, causing glandular fever. It can lay dormant in the body for long periods of time and when the conditions are right, it can re-emerge, multiply and cause symptoms. If the symptoms keep recurring, the body becomes depleted, ultimately leaving you feeling fatigued, run-down and unable to cope with daily life.

It is estimated that about 95% of the population have EBV in their system and most don't know about it. EBV has been linked to chronic fatigue syndrome. If you have had any past exposure to EBV and feel that your fatigue may be caused by it, a health practitioner will be able to provide you the help you need.

EBV is also labelled as a stealth infection due to its nature in the body and, in my experience, is the major contributor to the symptoms of the next section.

What Are Stealth Infections?

In my clinic I see stealth infections as a factor of long-term tiredness and fatigue issues in many of my clients. As the name suggests, stealth infections occurs when bacteria or viruses enter the cells of the body and cunningly hide to evade the immune system. Stealth infections can stay in the body for years as they slowly weaken the body and drain its nutrition and resources. It results in long-term inflammation and – because it is equivalent to stress – a long-term response by the adrenals.

When this process occurs for a long period of time – as it does with many undiagnosed stealth infections – a person will experience symptoms such as fatigue, brain fog, anaemia, food intolerances, allergies, hormonal imbalances, inability to cope, low stamina, or one day of feeling good and then the next two to three days of feeling quite wiped out.

Stealth infections are usually caused by cell wall deficient bacteria (resistant to most antibiotics), but they can also be viral, which can avoid the detection of the immune system and are undetectable by regular laboratory tests. These stealth infections linger over time and create toxins that can overwhelm your liver and rob you of nutrients. They can deplete the energy reactions inside your cells and allow other organisms to invade your already weakened body.

Examples of stealth infections include Epstein–Barr virus, mycoplasma, the herpes family of viruses, candida, hepatitis viruses, Helicobacter pylori, Giardia, Borrelia and Bartonella. The last two bacteria are linked to Lyme-like illnesses.

The problem with stealth infections is that the symptoms are quite generalised and can be missed if you are not aware of their effects. The symptoms are derived from the by-products or toxins of the infective agent. These toxins can overload the liver and the spleen (immune system) and cause generalised symptoms such as fatigue, brain fog, nervousness, tingling, dizziness, headaches, insomnia, irritable bowel symptoms, food sensitivities, memory loss, poor concentration, unrefreshed sleep and exhaustion.

The stronger your body and the better your nutrition, the less symptoms you'll experience. When your body is nutrient-depleted and overburdened due to chronic stress, poor lifestyle and food choices, or not having enough sleep, then the more severe the symptoms will be.

How Do I Know If I Have a Stealth Infection?

By looking back through your own health history. Have you or a close family member previously suffered from glandular fever virus, EBV, Ross River fever or infectious mononucleosis. These viruses can remain in the body as a latent or stealth infection. If you are unsure, get blood tests for EBV, Ross River virus, the herpes family, hepatitis and helicobacter. Ask your GP or trusted health practitioner to request these tests. Positive test results for a previous infection, could indicate a stealth infection causing your ongoing fatigue.

Other infective agents such as mycoplasma are not readily identified with laboratory tests. It's advisable to get as much information from testing as you can. Undergo blood tests that show your white blood cell count, liver enzymes inflammatory markers and cytokine markers to look at the whole picture. Other tests that can also identify if anything is amiss include vitamin D level, vitamin C status, zinc status and faecal stool analysis. Some stealth pathogens require specialised testing using DNA analysis to identify them.

Find a qualified health professional with experience in chronic infections to help you through this process.

There have been several of my clients who have been tested for the various infections and the results showed that there was a previous infection that was no longer active. Stealth infections can present themselves this way as they are hiding from the immune system.

I had a client who would be bedridden about every six months. Her energy would crash, she would be unable to work and would have to take six weeks off to recover. This cycle occurred about every six months for the last two years. I requested several blood tests to investigate previous or current exposure to viral infections. EBV presented itself, yet my client never recalled having the infection originally. The virus would go into stealth mode and then re-emerge when she became overworked and stressed from work. The treatment regime for her was to correct her nutrition, support her immune system and create a plan so that she didn't get to the point of overwork and overwhelm again. This helped her to recover and she was able to prevent the recurrent cycle of fatigue and was able to live her life to the fullest again.

In my clinic I use live blood microscopy to help with the process of looking for possible infective agents or signs of infective agents. Whilst the live blood microscopy cannot identify the pathogen, parameters of the blood can help point in the direction of which pathology test is needed next.

What Can You Do for Your Immune System?

There are several nutrients that are vital to strengthening your immune response.

- Vitamin D is more than just the sunlight vitamin; it acts as an antiviral and antibacterial agent, helps reduce your inflammatory response and aids your immune system. The best source of vitamin D is sunlight, just five to ten minutes per day of Australian sunlight during your lunch break is enough to boost your vitamin D production. Foods high in vitamin D include mushrooms exposed to sunlight before consuming, butter, wild-caught salmon, sardines, eggs and cod liver oil. Vitamin D can also be stored in the body as reserves.

- Vitamin C is required to help boost the function of your immune system and can help fight viral infections. Vitamin C cannot be stored in the body and so it is needed daily to have health benefits. Foods high in vitamin C include citrus foods, capsicum, kiwi fruit, pawpaw, berries, green leafy vegetables, broccoli, brussels sprouts, tomatoes, squash, potatoes (both sweet potato and white potato) and snow peas. Consume these foods daily to boost your vitamin C status.

- Zinc is a mineral that is used for over 300 enzymatic reactions in the body. It helps the immune system fight off invading bacteria and viruses. Good food sources of zinc include seafood, pepitas, nuts, seeds, meats, dairy, beans and legumes, and eggs.

As well as specific nutrients for the immune system, there are also many herbs that have been shown to have antiviral and antibacterial actions, as well as boosting the activity of the immune cells. I use many combinations of these in the clinic.

- Reishi, also known as Ganoderma, is a therapeutic mushroom that has been used for centuries in Asian cultures. It is revered as an adaptogen, helping the body to adapt to different circumstances. Traditionally, Reishi is used as a general tonic for deficiency syndromes associated with tiredness and fatigue. It has the ability to help support the immune system and has been shown to have antiviral actions.

- Cordyceps and Shiitake are two more therapeutic mushrooms that have beneficial effects on the immune system. They are both used in traditional Chinese medicine and have shown to have effects as antibacterial, antiviral and antiparasitic. Cordyceps can interact with pharmaceutical medications and should be used under professional advice. Shiitake can be purchased from your local green grocer or supermarket and used in cooking.

- Astragalus is an herb used with great respect in traditional Chinese medicine. This herb stimulates the immune function and has benefits in the treatment of viral infections. It has been prescribed for centuries to treat chronic illnesses and general weakness, as well as to help increase vitality and build stamina.

- Andrographis has been used in India for centuries to treat infections such as malaria, syphilis and recurrent influenza. It is also used to treat Lyme disease and herpes viral infections (both stealth infections). This herb can be used in a formulation with other immune system enhancing herbs to help with chronic infections. Beware that some people can get an allergic rash or hives after taking this herb.

Other herbs that possess antiviral, antibacterial or antiparasitic actions include Isatis, Goldenseal, Lomatium, Garlic, Cat's claw, Sida, Holy Basil, Olive leaf, Usnea and Japanese Knotweed. In my clinic I use herbal formulations with a combination of some of these herbs depending upon the symptom picture of the client.

Take Action Now

Look into whether chronic infections are the cause of your fatigue. Get a blood test to identify your vitamin D and C status, investigate possible viral and bacterial infections, get a white blood cell count, and inflammatory markers, such as high sensitivity, C-reactive protein (CRP), erythrocyte sedimentation rate (ESR) and cytokine markers.

If you find out that you have a viral infection or a chronic bacterial infection, it's not the end of the world. Simply take steps to strengthen your general nutrition, support your liver and digestive system as we have already addressed. Consult with a naturopath for a regime of nutrients and herbs to optimise your immune system and restore your nutrition.

It does take time, and it will not be an overnight success, but rest assured it will help restore your energy and help you restore your fabulous self. You will feel better again.

7. Energy Robbers

'What you do each day or the people in your life will either drain your energy or help your energy. Choose well.'

– Teressa Todd

Everyday foods, routines and habits can rob you of your daily energy, with or without you realising it. They can leave you feeling fatigued, drained and exhausted. By identifying your energy robbers, you can limit their effect on you and the drain that they place on your life. Once these are eliminated, you can restore your energy, have better clarity of thought, be able to cope easier with daily pressures and regain your vitality once again.

Energy robbers can create a rollercoaster ride of ups and downs in your energy. Some energy robbers can sneak up on you and you don't notice them happening, others you feel very quickly but don't know what to do. Have you ever had a coffee and felt great for one to two hours, only to feel tired and grumpy again a couple of hours later, then look for the next energy hit? Have you had an interaction with someone and then afterwards felt absolutely wiped out? By observing your body and how foods, routines, events and people affect you, you can identify your energy robbers.

What Are Energy Robbers?

They can be everyday habits, activities, foods, people or situations that can create a negative response in your body to drain your energy.

Let's think of the energy in your body in terms of water in a bucket. The water in the bucket can be lost through evaporation, by someone drinking it, or holes at the side of the bucket letting the water leak out. If any of these occur consistently, then the water in the bucket will decrease and eventually there will be nothing left. Now in your bucket, it is energy rather than water. If there are incidents that occur and drain you daily, then your bucket of energy will diminish. If your energy bucket is only half full to start with – due to the demands of the modern woman – then the energy robbers will drain out the bucket quicker.

Energy robbers that you could experience include:

- refined sugar
- caffeine
- processed foods
- stress
- alcohol
- illicit drugs
- some pharmaceutical medications
- technology devices such as mobile phones, computers, iPads, tablets and televisions
- late nights and not enough sleep

- chemical and toxin exposure

- even your own negative thoughts going around in your head

- an interaction with a person that leaves you feeling depleted afterwards

Refined Sugar

When you consume refined sugar, it is absorbed into your system and increases your blood glucose level. When you have high blood sugar levels, you experience an energy burst, like going down on a rollercoaster. The body has safeguards in place for when the blood sugar level reaches outside of a specific range. When this happens, the pancreas produces insulin – the vehicle that takes the glucose into the cells to be metabolised or takes it to the liver to be converted into a different form called glycogen for storage.

When your blood sugar increases too quickly and the pancreas produces too much insulin, it will cause your blood sugar levels to drop quickly, causing you to crash. With this crash, you can experience tiredness, fatigue, foggy thought, shakiness and headaches.

If you regularly consume refined sugar and continually have high blood sugar level and a high need for insulin, you can become insulin resistant.

Insulin resistance is a condition whereby the cells no longer become responsive to insulin, leading to metabolic syndrome. Irritability, weight gain and fatigue are some of the symptoms that are associated with this condition. The good news is that you can avoid refined sugars and easily find replacements that you can enjoy instead without the blood sugar rollercoaster ride. Most processed foods contain some form of sugar. Eating a diet based on salad, fruits and vegetables will give you the nutrition you need for your energy and help your body create the energy it needs. Eating a balanced diet full of nutrients actually helps to reduce the need or want for sugary foods.

Many times in my clinic I prescribe an eating plan based on salad, fruits and vegetables with portions of protein and good fats. After implementing this for a few weeks, my clients say that they have better overall energy, are less likely to want sugary foods and don't feel good when they do eat sweets.

Refined sugar contributes to nutrient depletion. The sugar-laden foods do not generally provide much nutrition and instead require nutrients from your body to metabolise the sugar, leaving you feeling irritated and fatigued.

Since sugar is addictive it can be hard for some to cut it out of their diet. That is why my approach is to build up the nutrition of the client first through eating plans and then address the sugar consumption a couple weeks later.

For healthy snacks, use dates, honey, carrots and apples in recipes. For sugar alternatives, there are many recipes available for whole food desserts or snacks online. A book that I recommend to clients is *Eat Desserts for Breakfast* by Nicole Joy.

Still want more ideas? Visit *www.teressatodd.com* to download snack ideas. Go to resources tab and use code word FABULOUS for access.

Once you have reduced or cut out altogether the refined sugar, you will feel more stable in energy and mood and have clearer thought.

Caffeine

It is commonly known that caffeine stimulates the brain and its effect can last for a couple of hours. You are probably thinking, 'Then how can it be an energy robber?' Well, at the same time, caffeine triggers the adrenals to produce adrenaline. When the adrenaline energy burst wears off, you feel fatigued and tired again. If the adrenals are already burdened from constant stress, then over time the caffeine will contribute to long-term fatigue. If you drink coffee constantly, you will need larger doses of coffee to get the same stimulation effect.

Not only does caffeine cause a high and a low as refined sugar does, but it also depletes your B group vitamins. It places a load on the liver for detoxification and it reduces your ability to absorb many nutrients, including iron, zinc and magnesium, all of which are vital to create energy.

As with sugar, caffeine is addictive – stopping coffee or energy drinks will trigger withdrawal symptoms, such as headaches, tremors, aches and pains.

Some of my clients say that they cannot stop their coffee intake as they need it to function. Similar to sugar cravings, it is best to begin with nutrition and use herbs to help restore the energy, then gradually reduce your coffee intake, rather than going cold turkey. You could start by reducing the number of cups of coffee, or you could reduce the strength of each cup of coffee. There are also great alternatives to coffee – Tea Tonic has a coffee addict tea that helps kick the coffee habit.

Once you restore your nutrition and support your adrenals, you will find that you won't need caffeine as much. If you can't stop coffee for four weeks, then look to reduce your caffeine intake slowly over time.

Alcohol

Alcohol can contribute to the fatigue feeling. Alcohol initially makes you feel relaxed when you first drink it, but after an hour or two, or usually the next day, you will feel tired and groggy. You will then need more caffeine and more sugar to counteract that groggy feeling, hence you unintentionally perpetuate the energy robbing cycle. Alcohol is metabolised in your liver and requires several nutrients, including B group vitamins that are needed for your energy production. It also affects your blood sugar metabolism and puts you on that high and low cycle again, so you get a double whammy.

Many people tend to use alcohol to wind down in the afternoon or evening. Start by using another method to help yourself unwind. Use a cup of relaxing herbal tea while watching the sunset or play relaxing music on the way home. Cutting alcohol will help you feel more energised the following day. Try eliminating alcohol for four weeks to rediscover your vibrant energy.

Technology

Technology is one of the energy robbers that we tend to overlook, because it's always around us. Sitting in front of a computer will contribute to your fatigue. When you are on technology such as a computer for long periods of time, your circulation slows down, your blinking rate reduces, and your eyes dry out a bit more. The light from the screen creates an oxidative reaction on your eyes, which is equivalent to a rusting process. Sitting in a chair with your arms perched in a typing position is not a natural posture and places strain on your neck, shoulder and back muscles. Blood circulation is reduced, and fatigue sets in.

Think about a time when you had to sit in front of computer all day for work and how low you felt when you got up. I know if I have a lot of computer work to do, I will feel a lot more exhausted than if I spent the day running after my children.

Electronic devices emit blue light which affects our melatonin production and can play havoc with the quality of our sleep. These digital devices also steal time from you without you realising it. Have you ever watched a movie and not realised that two hours have gone by? Have you ever been on social media without realising that you've been on there for an hour when you only intended to take a quick five minutes look?

This was the case with one of my clients, Jo. She was a bright, fun-loving woman in her late 20s with an autoimmune disease – fatigue was one of her presenting symptoms. Jo worked long hours and had long travelling times to and from work. With such a packed week, she didn't get to see her friends regularly, so at night she would try to catch up through social media. She would spent two to three hours on social media late into the night without even realising it. This was eating into her sleep time and the blue light from the phone wasn't allowing her to create the melatonin needed to encourage good quality sleep, which aggravated her autoimmune disease. As part of the recovery process, I recommended that she set a timer or an alarm whenever she was on social media. That way she didn't lose concept of time and could go to bed earlier to get the nourishing sleep she needed to function the next day.

If you use social media and often lose track of time, set a timer for fifteen minutes to remind yourself to get off and out of that rabbit hole. You could then go back again later in the day, so it's not all in one chunk. Doing small, bite sized pieces will definitely help with how you're feeling.

If you need to be on a computer for your work, take regular breaks to get up and move about. Set an alarm to move about each hour. Get up, take a brief walk around the office, do some stretches and take some deep relaxing breaths. Look at how you can structure your work day to rotate between a short burst of screen time and another activity that doesn't use a screen. Additionally, blue light reducing glasses can be used during the times that you are on a computer or laptop; these can be found easily online.

Negative Self-Talk

Let's look at the thoughts – especially negative thoughts – that are going on in your head and how they can become energy robbers. Negative thoughts, or stressful thoughts, can be draining emotionally and mentally especially when the negative thoughts are like a mouse wheel – just going around and around and around. This can leave you feeling more fatigued and worn out.

Negative thoughts are the ones where you think that you are not doing a good job as a mum or feel guilty because of something that has happened in one of your relationships. It is common for mums to put pressure on themselves – pressure of not being good enough, forgetting to pick up something from the shops, pressure to keep everything in order and being seen as the perfect mum, wife, employee or friend. This is the 'Supermum' image. I think that every mum is a Supermum in their own right, just doing what we do. We do not have to put extra pressure on ourselves trying to achieve an idealised image we created in our minds.

Negative thoughts can come from our own pressures, thinking of the worst-case scenarios for events that may not even happen. Do you think about situations that may or may not occur in the future and think through various scenario endings and what you can do in each scenario?

These negative thoughts – no matter where they originate – create a stress response from the adrenals. If these negative thoughts are continual, it can lead to adrenal burnout, resulting in fatigue and lack of motivation.

The trick is to be aware of your thoughts and stop the negative ones before they create a stress response in your body. The act of stopping thoughts, redirecting and being in the present moment takes practice and patience. Think of the thoughts as children who sometimes misbehave. As a parent you would try to direct the child to better behaviour. Treat your thoughts the same way.

Tips to Change Negative Self-Talk

Use the following tips to guide your thoughts and break the cycle of negative thoughts going through your head.

1. Keep a gratitude diary to record and think about the positive things in your life. Bringing positive thoughts to your awareness will help to crowd out the consistent negative thoughts and spare your adrenals from the stress response.

2. If you have a thought going around and around in circles, be aware of it. Use your power of thought to change the

pattern and actively think of something positive, or visualise the event or thing going well. If it is something that you need to do, make a note to come back to it at a later time when you can deal with it. If it is a thought that may never happen, write it down to your future self and then leave the thoughts on the paper.

3. Be in the present moment. If you are driving, actively concentrate on what is going on around you. If you are making dinner, actively think about each step. Be in that moment. I sometimes find my mind racing when I am hanging clothes on the clothes line. So, I concentrate on picking up the pegs, placing the clothes nicely over the line and then pegging them. During this time, I am aware of the birds chirping in the big tree behind our house and how lovely they sound. A much better way to spend time on a mundane job than thinking of the things I have to do the rest of the day, or that the kids didn't pick up the clothes off their floor when I asked.

You may think, how does changing my thinking change my fatigue and my life? When we stop the continual negative thoughts that are going on in the mind, we can stop the constant stress response which drains our energy. Then we can utilise the energy we create in more productive processes, such as healing our body, and utilising our nutrition for repair and vitality.

If the negative thoughts are overwhelming and you struggle to take control of them, then seek out strategies or advice from a professional to change and release them.

Energy Vampires

Just as your own negative thoughts can be an energy robber, people can do the same. A term that's used to describe people who are energy robbers is 'Energy Vampire'.

When you interact with an energy vampire you can be left feeling flat, frazzled and fatigued. It is not necessarily intentional on their behalf. I recently spoke with a client who was in a situation where a cousin was needing emotional help. While my client was happy to help, each interaction left her feeling more tired, stressed out and uneasy. She was already in a fatigued state and these interactions were depleting her markedly. We discussed options that she could do to protect herself. She was unable to leave a family member in distress, so we decided that the time spent with the cousin should be short in duration and afterwards my client would spend some time doing something else to refill her energy back again. She likes to paint, so it was suggested that she spend some time painting after each encounter with her cousin.

Your energy vampire may be a friend or an acquaintance and it is best to limit or avoid these people while you are restoring your energy and building yourself up to full health. The energy vampire may be your boss or a close family member and you can't just say, 'Hey, I don't want to spend time with you.' Instead you might discuss with the person how you are feeling, that you're working on yourself to restore your energy and that you need some extra space to rebuild your energy. If discussions with this person are not an option, then try to limit the direct contact time with them. Use some relaxing breathing techniques to restore your calm and vigour and vitality, or use laughter, if it's appropriate, to help lighten the mood and the stress response after being in their company. If this doesn't work, look to get some strategies from a counsellor to help you in that specific situation.

Action Time

Listen to your body and feel what happens after certain activities, after interactions with certain people, when you eat certain foods, or drink alcohol. Keep a diary to help you identify your immediate or potential energy robbers and make a plan to reduce or eliminate them. This will give you a clearer picture of what needs to be addressed first.

Start with one item at a time. Look at your life and schedule and pick one thing to change each week. Change can be challenging, just start with one easy task and work your way up from there. Write down which one of these energy robbers you could address first without feeling overwhelmed and commit to that for the next week.

One strategy would be to look at technology first and then move to alcohol and sugar. Limit your screen time on your mobile phones, computers and television. Allow yourself a fixed amount of time to be on these devices, and turn them off before bedtime and keep them out of your bedroom, so they don't disrupt you during the night and tempt you to get on social media if you wake up in the middle of the night.

By identifying the aspects of your life that drain your energy, you can choose to take action and start to restore your energy, reduce your fatigue and feel fabulous again.

8. Magic Herbs and Nutrients

'Let food be thy medicine and medicine be thy food.'

– Hippocrates

Food and nutrition are the cruxes to your energy and vitality. Without proper nutrition, the body cannot create the energy it needs for healthy functioning, you become fatigued and run-down. The body has an amazing way of healing itself and creating the energy we need, it just needs the right ingredients and nutrients.

This chapter is named Magic Herbs and Nutrients, because many of my clients, whom I have provided individualised herbal formula and addressed their nutritional health deficiencies, returned after only a month to say that they're feeling great, they're energised, they're motivated, they're able to take on all the tasks of their day and have extra energy for their kids afterwards.

Food and nutrients, including herbs, communicate to our genes giving them instructions about how to function and respond to our environment. From this information, the genes create enzymes and proteins that drive all bodily functions in the body. If your food is poor in nutrition or lacks enough good quality nutrients, the genetic function will be affected.

Think of this in terms of a business. If the cash flow and productivity reports that the boss receives are not correct, then all future decisions and instructions from the boss will be inaccurate for what is needed for a flourishing business. The productivity and cash flow of the business will not match the demand and eventually the business fails.

Key nutrients are like the reports, they drive the genes (boss) and this in turn creates the cellular reactions within the body (decisions and instructions). When the correct instructions from the genes are given, the body is better able to deal with stress, have clearer thought, be able to take on new challenges and have better motivation and stamina.

Good Nutrition Drives Your Cellular Energy

Inside our cells, an organelle called the mitochondria creates adenosine triphosphate (ATP), otherwise known as energy. The ATP produced by the mitochondria is not only an energy source for the cells but acts as a catalyst for other reactions and processes in the body. To create ATP, the mitochondria uses a biochemical cycle called the citric acid cycle. Let's cut the biochemistry lesson short and just note that there are certain nutrients that the chemical reactions of this cycle need in order to create ATP. Knowing this you can consume foods high in specific nutrients, such as carbohydrates, fats and protein, zinc, vitamin B1, vitamin B2, vitamin B3, vitamin B5, magnesium, manganese and iron.

Let's look into these specific nutrients, I am not going to concentrate too much on the macronutrients which are protein, carbohydrates and fats. Packaged food will list these nutrients and give a value of how much is present in that food product. As these macronutrients contribute calories to our body, many diets – especially weight loss diets – will concentrate on the number of calories that you are consuming. If you are on a calorie-restricted diet, then you will be counting the calories in your diet. Now the calories are not the same for each macronutrient. Carbohydrates and protein generate 4 calories per gram each and fat generates 9 calories per gram.

Why am I telling you this science? You need to understand that weight loss diets and calorie-counting does not necessarily work long-term (due to cheat days) and can wreak havoc on your energy cycles. I do not talk in terms of calorie-counting with my clients as I have seen many who have been given a set number of calories to eat per day and chose to eat a Tim Tam over a handful of pepitas because it fits the calorie target per day. They did not realise that the pepitas contain zinc and magnesium which are vital for their citric acid cycle. These clients find themselves feeling fatigued and tired because they're not giving their body all the correct nutrients needed to create energy.

There are all kinds of diets around – high fat, low fat, high protein, greens and protein only, low carbohydrate, etc. There is no universal diet that works for everyone and some of these diets can leave you feeling dazed, confused, unmotivated and fatigued instead.

Whilst the macronutrients such as carbohydrates, proteins and fats are needed to provide your calories, let's go beyond the macronutrients and take a closer look at the micronutrients that are needed for the cellular reactions to occur inside the cells.

Important Micronutrients

Micronutrients are essential vitamins and minerals vital to our cellular reactions. Vitamins and minerals help the body release the energy that's stored in the food we eat. We cannot manufacture them, so we need to harness it from food. When nutrients are crucial to the cellular reactions of the body, they are called cofactors. Many micronutrients are cofactors.

Let's look at these key micronutrients.

Iron

Iron is important for many aspects of the body and you've already probably heard about iron deficiency, anaemia and the resulting fatigue that comes from that. Iron is an essential mineral for maintaining your optimal energy and stamina and is involved in the transportation of oxygen in the red blood cells, muscle function, brain function, and it is also involved in your immunity and nervous system.

When you're deficient you may experience shortness of breath, chronic dull headaches, poor memory and concentration, dizziness, fatigue, palpitations on exertion, paleness of your skin, restless legs, poor immunity and muscle aches and pains.

You can become deficient in iron if you are not consuming food rich in iron, or if your digestive system is not digesting your food and absorbing them correctly. I covered the importance of good digestive functioning in Chapter 1.

Food intolerances and intestinal flora imbalances can also contribute to low iron absorption. Women with heavy menstrual flow can also be low in iron because of the extra blood loss.

Good sources of iron include beef, lamb, chicken, eggs, oysters, sardines, almonds, apricots, parsley, pine nuts, avocado, sunflower, pumpkin seeds and dark green leafy veggies. A variety of food is important so that you can maximise your iron absorption from these foods.

A simple way to test your iron is to get an iron studies test done through a pathology lab. The iron studies test will check more than just the iron levels in your blood, it also shows your ability to bind the iron and checks your body's iron stores.

If you think you are low in iron, don't just rush out and get an iron supplement, get tested first. There is a condition called iron overload, as well as a genetic condition called hemochromatosis. This is where your body stores too much iron and the symptoms can be similar to iron deficiency. An iron studies test can check your iron to determine whether your iron is too high or too low.

If you are deficient in iron, you may need to supplement your body with a good quality absorbable iron to increase your levels quickly and restore your energy fast. Relying on food alone can take several months to really build up that iron store, so in my clinic I recommend iron supplements that don't cause constipation and are easily absorbable for maximum results.

Magnesium

Magnesium is another mineral that is vital for energy production. Magnesium is involved in over 300 chemical reactions in the body and it is a cofactor that is necessary to form and store ATP.

Other uses for magnesium are protein synthesis, muscle and nerve function, regulation of blood sugar, as well as reducing inflammation in the body. This mineral is required to help your muscles relax. When you are in a state of constant stress, your muscles are primed for contraction to run away, using up vital magnesium.

It is estimated about 30% of Australian adults are deficient in magnesium and assessing true magnesium levels is difficult. Unlike iron, blood testing for magnesium is not accurate. It doesn't show the level of magnesium inside the cells or in the cerebral spinal fluid, where it's crucial. A combination of salivary, urinary and blood test for magnesium will give a true indication of your magnesium levels.

Symptoms of magnesium deficiency can include muscular cramps, insulin resistance, anxiety, cold hands, cold feet, fatigue, blood sugar irregularities, depression, insomnia, palpitations, easily startled and jumpy, poor appetite, premenstrual tension and vertigo.

Food sources of magnesium include almonds, cashews, macadamias, walnuts, brazil nuts, pine nuts, pecans, pistachios, cacao, eggs, figs, green leafy veggies, sunflower seeds, sesame seeds, apricots, apples, dates, prunes, bananas, spinach, parsley, shallots, legumes and coconut water.

Food is a great source for magnesium but sometimes it's not absorbed well enough. For many of my clients I recommend a magnesium or Epsom salt bath or footbath to help improve their magnesium levels as we can absorb this mineral through our skin. Relaxing with your feet soaking in an Epsom salt foot bath while watching a comedy movie or reading a good book is great ME time.

In some cases, good quality magnesium supplementation is required to increase the levels quicker. Not all magnesium supplements are equal in their ability to be absorbed. For absorption, magnesium is bound to carrier molecules. These carrier molecules can change how the magnesium is absorbed and the effect the magnesium has on the body. For instance, magnesium oxide is not well absorbed and tends to cause diarrhoea. While magnesium chelate or glycinate are far easier to absorb and can help replenish cellular levels.

Zinc

This mineral is essential to every cellular reaction of the body. Let's call it the 'super mineral'. Zinc is required as a cofactor for your energy production, it is involved in the digestive enzymes, immune function, taste and smell, DNA replication, and muscle function and repair.

Symptoms of zinc deficiency include low energy, white spots of fingernails, loss of appetite, slow wound healing, recurrent infections, skin conditions such as acne and scarring, altered taste and smell, hormonal imbalances and poor memory.

Food sources are a great way to improve your zinc status – such as pepitas, beans, lean meats, nuts, fish and other seafood. Zinc supplementation can be used if needed, but it is best to check your zinc levels with a blood test and monitor your zinc as it can interfere with your copper and iron absorption

B Vitamins – The Energy Vitamins

The B group vitamins are a group of vitamins that are essential to the body for energy production and cell metabolism. They are water-soluble vitamins, meaning that we do not store them and whatever we don't use we excrete through our urine.

Many of the B group vitamins can be destroyed by heat, light exposure and the length of time it takes to get the food source from the farm to the plate. Eating a variety of fresh, seasonal foods – both cooked and raw – is vital to getting sufficient amounts of the B group vitamins.

- Vitamin B1, or thiamine, is an essential vitamin that aids the conversion of carbohydrates into energy and is involved in the normal functioning of our heart, muscles and nervous systems. Good food sources for vitamin B1 are potatoes, sunflower seeds, sesame seeds, tahini, hummus, oatmeal, peanuts, some dairy products, whole grain foods, soy milk, lean meats, sunflower seeds and dried beans.

- Vitamin B2, or riboflavin, plays a vital role in the metabolism of proteins, fats and carbohydrates, and the formation of red blood cells. It also plays a vital role in maintaining the body's energy. Good sources of vitamin B2 include eggs, almonds, oysters, raw broccoli, parsley, dark green leafy vegetables, fish, lean meat, cheese and mushrooms.

- Vitamin B3, or niacin, is involved in the metabolism of carbohydrates, proteins and fats, and their conversion into energy. It is also involved in the production of stress hormones from the adrenal glands and aids in the detoxification of toxins through the liver. This vitamin can be made from an amino acid called tryptophan or can be sourced in foods such as cottage cheese, fish, legumes, lean meats, nuts, poultry, eggs, sunflower seeds and green leafy vegetables.

- Vitamin B6, or pyridoxine, is essential as a cofactor for many of the energy reactions in our body. It plays a role in brain and nervous system health, and is involved in the production of the mood hormone (serotonin), stress hormone (norepinephrine) and sleep hormone (melatonin). Vitamin B6 also plays a role in the healthy function of the immune system. Food sources of vitamin B6 are sunflower seeds, bananas, spinach, fish, green beans, meats and eggs. Beware though, long-term supplementation of this vitamin in high doses can cause nerve damage.

- Folic acid has a reputation for being the pregnancy vitamin. Beyond pregnancy, it has more far-reaching health effects. Folate and folic acid are also known as vitamin B9 and are involved in the health of gene replication, reduction in the inflammatory chemical homocysteine, aids in red blood cell formation and acts as vital cofactor, just like B6, for energy production. Rich sources of folate are green leafy vegetables, broccoli, cauliflower, cabbage, egg, parsnips, citrus fruits, tomatoes, chicken, shellfish and legumes.

- Vitamin B12, or cobalamin, is key for energy production. When you are low in vitamin B12 you feel tired and have difficulty with thought. Along with folate, it helps reduce the inflammatory chemical called homocysteine. This vitamin is vital to the health of the nerve cells and their covering, the myelin sheath. Good levels of vitamin B12 helps brain neurotransmitters which in turn helps elevate your moods. Food sources of vitamin B12 are mainly animal products such as meat, chicken, fish, dairy and eggs. It is a vitamin that the beneficial bacteria in the intestines can manufacture, but we need good levels of the beneficial bacteria in the gut in order to do this for us.

The above information is to show you how important each of the B vitamins are and how they all have their specific function in supporting the health of the body. Although we've gone into each of these individually, it is always best to use B vitamins as a group of vitamins. They all interact in relation to each other, so if you are thinking of taking a supplement, use a vitamin B complex rather than individual vitamins. While food sources are always the best, there are some occasions where supplementation will help to improve your levels, support your adrenals, and balance mood and energy faster.

Phytochemicals – The Unsung Heroes

Besides the macro and micronutrients, foods also contain phytochemicals that communicate with your genes and enhance cellular activity. Unlike vitamins and minerals, phytochemicals are not essential to the functioning of the body, but instead can help optimise cellular reactions.

Phytochemicals are produced in plants as part of their defence mechanism, usually against insects or disease, and it provides the colour and flavour to the food we eat. There have been thousands of phytochemicals discovered and more of them are continually being discovered every day.

Phytochemicals have a myriad of actions and they can help in the crusade against tiredness and fatigue. Some actions of phytochemicals include antioxidants, such as resveratrol in grapes and dark chocolate. Antioxidants promote heart health and has anti-cancer properties. Other phytochemicals – such as allicin found in garlic – have an antimicrobial action, meaning they can help to kill bacteria, viruses or other pathogens.

Some phytochemicals can influence genetic expression and therefore help with proper functioning of the genes for health. An example of this is quercetin in onions which helps reduce inflammation in our body. Sulforaphane is a compound in broccoli; there is a lot of research in the role it plays in liver detoxification pathways, anti-cancer and hormone balance.

The bottom line that you can take from this is that there are many compounds in food that science is yet to determine fully. These compounds or phytochemicals communicate with the genes to promote health and vitality. Since phytochemicals are involved in colour and flavour of food, I suggest that you use a lot of colour and variety of flavours in your meals so it ensures you are getting a plethora of phytochemicals, and in turn get a variety of essential nutrients such as B vitamins, zinc and magnesium, as well as countless other phytochemical nutrients. As a result, it will support your body, energy, health and moods.

Make salad, fruits and veggies the hero of your plate. Your plate should be filled two-thirds with salad, fruits and vegetables, include lots of colour and variety – greens, reds, yellows, blue-blacks and whites. The remaining third of the plate can be a mix of beans, legumes, meat, chicken, fish or grain alternatives.

Herbs

Herbs work most effectively in our body with the help of phytochemicals. Medicinal herbs are plants that contain specific phytochemicals that promote health. Just as in food, the herbs are able to help with the functioning of cellular reactions.

In my opinion, herbs are more potent in their effect in providing health benefits than food. There are hundreds of years of evidence to support this as well. Many traditional cultures valued certain plants for their ability to support health and well-being. For example, during World War II, Russian soldiers used herbs to help with their stamina and endurance. Whilst there are thousands of medicinal herbs available for a variety of conditions, in this section we're just going to look at the herbs that have an adaptogenic property and support the stress response and your overall energy.

Many herbs are referred to as adaptogens. This means that it is a natural substance that helps to normalise and regulate reactions in the body and, as the name suggests, helps the body to adapt to stress.

In this modern world of countless stresses, adaptogens are the key to help the body cope with the constant demands, pressures and insults. Herbs can help the body change the way it reacts to the constant stressors.

Keep in mind that herbs should always be prescribed by a qualified herbal practitioner, as there can be unintended interactions with other medications if you are not careful. In my clinic, I use a selection of the following herbs as part of a treatment plan to help support the client's ability to adapt to their current life situation and pressures. The selection of herbs is catered to individual clients as they each come to me with a different presenting complaint.

- Cordyceps is a traditional Chinese herb that is great for increasing physical stamina and energy. In 1993 Chinese female athletes broke nine world records at the Chinese national games and it was revealed that they were using Cordyceps as part of their training regime to help their body adapt to the demands of training. Science has shown that this herb can increase your cellular energy or ATP and it is used by many herbalists to help with symptoms of mental fog, fatigue and dizziness. It can also help improve the immune system function.

- Reishi is another traditional Chinese herb, also known as Ganoderma. Traditionally, it was used by the Taoist monks to promote centred calmness, improve their meditation practices and attain a long, healthy life. Reishi is known as a relaxing adaptogen, so it can help a person adapt to stress while relaxing the body. In my clinic I have used this herb and clients have shown great results in their energy, fatigue and recurrent infections. It can help to reduce inflammation, balance the immune system, protect the liver and nervous system. These actions can make it very helpful in many conditions associated with fatigue.

- Holy Basil is an Indian herb that is revered as the Queen of Herbs. Many scientific studies are showing what Ayurvedic medicine has known for a long time. Holy Basil is an adaptogenic herb that can help with stressful environments and can help calm the anxious person. As with many herbs, Holy Basil needs to be used with caution as it can interact with other medications.

- Rhodiola is another favourite herb. Many of my clients come back to me and say that they feel less stressed and more capable of dealing with everyday situations. This herb is an adaptogen, helping to modify a person's response to stress. Traditionally, this herb is known to build stamina, strength and vitality in harsh climates and has been used to treat fatigue and depression. It can also help with memory and concentration – something that every busy mum needs.

- Siberian Ginseng is an herb that I use when a client needs an energy lift and has very little reserves left. This herb can help with general fatigue and tiredness, and especially when there is insomnia present. It is a restorative tonic for physical and mental weakness and can help with the recovery from intense and stressful situations. Scientific studies have shown that this herb can help improve the mental work capacity during stressful situations, meaning that the person can think better in situations of high stress.

- Nearly every tonic I formulate will include an herb called Withania as part of the formula. This is an Indian Ayurvedic herb also known as Ashwagandha or Indian Ginseng. Withania promotes physical and mental health in adverse conditions and increases one's resilience to stress. Like Rhodiola, Withania can help promote a person's memory and adaptation to stress.

- Schisandra has many actions, but it's commonly used by the Chinese to treat fatigue and memory issues. This herb is also known to promote longevity and help with physical, mental stamina and stress response.

- An Indian herb called Brahmi, or Bacopa, has great adaptogenic action in strengthening the brain and the mind. In Sanskrit, *Brahmi* means to expand the consciousness. This herb can help when you have a mentally demanding job or poor memory. I can personally recommend this herb for its ability to help memory and recall in a stressful situation. I came across this herb while I was studying my second university degree and decided to use it. I found that my memory and my recall was so much better than during my first degree, and yet I had the same study techniques.

Herbs can be used as an addition to help your body cope with an environment that is constantly demanding, especially for a mother. Seek qualified herbal advice before taking these, as many of these herbs can interact with other medications.

Patience is needed to restore your energy and allow your body to heal itself. Your body needs specific nutrients for proper functioning but also needs time for the repair process. Herbs and nutrients are not magic pills that work overnight. Some of the results can take several weeks before they become evident. Work with a health professional that can guide you through your health journey back to your fabulous self.

Your Action Plan

Get an assessment of where your nutrition is at. Find a qualified health professional that can help you test your nutrition status and find out which foods and nutrients you need to support your cellular health.

Check your diet if you're getting a good quality and variety of salad, fruits and veggies. Ensure that you're getting a minimum of three to four cups of salad, fruits and vegetables per day, with as much colour and variety as you can.

The phytochemicals in herbs can help your body adapt to the current stresses and demands that your body is experiencing. This may help quicken the restoration of your energy, clearer thought and moods, and better adaptation to stress. Ask a qualified herbalist for the best suited herbs for your situation.

9. Sleep Easy Solutions

'Sleep is that golden chain that ties health and our bodies together.'

– Thomas Dekker

We all know that a good night's sleep helps reduce fatigue, restore energy and vitality, but for so many it is a struggle to get good quality sleep without any interruption. Sleep is the most important way to recharge your body. It is vital to helping your body to repair and to heal itself.

Good sleep helps you to cope better with the stresses and strains of everyday life, you will have clearer thinking, better memory and better problem-solving capabilities. Furthermore, you will feel happier, be more patient with yourself and with others, and be able to take on each day with vigour. When we don't get enough sleep, we have a slower reaction time that can actually contribute to traffic accidents, work accidents and many other errors in our day.

Sleep is an intrinsic part to your body's healing process. The body is designed to sleep during dark times of the night and wake up with sunrise. Artificial light, modern technology and stresses, stop you from being able to switch off and sleep well. By using a few key strategies, you can improve the quality of your sleep and ensure you have adequate energy and clarity to power through each day. This way you will wake up feeling refreshed and invigorated, ready for the new day.

Sleep is a critical part of everyday life, no different from eating and drinking. You may mistakenly think that it's where the body just shuts down for several hours, as a computer does. Science has shown that sleep is an active time. During this time, you are solidifying and creating neural connections for the day's memories. It is a time that you create growth hormones to help grow and repair tissues and muscles. Adequate sleep also helps your emotions and how you view the world, so when you're tired, small things tend to feel like large things and you're unable to cope with them. You feel more on edge and you have a shorter fuse, unable to actually think clearly. This will contribute to your fatigue and lack of motivation, but when you get adequate, good quality sleep you'll feel vital and energised.

Studies have also shown that good sleep helps to reduce the risk of depression, anxiety, chronic disease and even cancers.

How Much Sleep Do I Need?

There is no set rule to how much sleep someone needs. On average it's estimated the adult human requires about seven to nine hours of sleep. I have some clients who are very capable with only five hours of sleep and they wake up feeling refreshed, whereas others need to have a solid eight to nine hours, anything less and they feel like walking zombies during the day.

Limit any daytime naps to less than thirty minutes if you struggle to fall asleep at night. Sleeping through the day can interrupt the circadian rhythm and cause you to struggle in the evenings.

The Sleep Hormone

Let's think about how your body was designed and how it works. We were designed to have an environment where we go to sleep just after dark and we might only have a low light available such as a small fire. In darkness the pineal gland in the brain produces a hormone called melatonin. This hormone initiates your sleep and contributes to the quality of sleep during the night. Melatonin is only ever produced in a dark environment.

In the current era of electricity and artificial lights, it is not unusual to have rooms lit with brightness until bedtime. The modern technology of LED lights and the blue light that comes from our computers and smartphones stop the production of melatonin. When you are sitting up at night watching television, on your mobile phone scrolling through social media, or reading and answering e-mails, you are not able to produce the melatonin you need to tell your body that it is time to go to sleep. If you go to bed after doing these tasks, you can find yourself awake for hours. I have clients who then decide that it is better to stay up later watching television or on their computer in the hopes that they will become more tired. Instead the bright light is keeping them awake.

If you struggle to go to sleep, help your body make melatonin by turning off computers, mobile phones, televisions and bright lights, then relax in a dimly lit environment for about an hour before bedtime. Listen to an audiobook or relaxing music, or use this time to meditate.

Some clients say that watching television is their relaxing time before bed, it is the only time that mums get to themselves after they have put their kids to bed, they can't switch off without it. My suggestion is to try other relaxing activities first – listen to an audiobook or some music. If this doesn't work, then watch television for a shorter amount of time but use blue light reducing glasses. Investing in the relaxing time before bed will help you feel more energetic and vitalised the next day.

Foods can help your body produce melatonin, such as nuts, seeds, cheese, red meat, chicken, turkey, fish, oats, beans, lentils, eggs and tofu. Consume them throughout the afternoon and evening. Tart or sour cherry juice is another good source of melatonin and I encourage my clients to drink 50 ml about an hour before bed.

If sleep is a problem for you it is best to check your cortisol and melatonin levels, and this can be done using a saliva test. High cortisol and low melatonin levels will prevent you from getting your refreshing sleep. Find a good practitioner to request this testing and they can help you identify if you need to boost your melatonin levels.

Steps for Bedtime

If you are having trouble relaxing into sleep, create a set bedtime. Avoid regular late nights that cause sleep debt – trying to catch up on sleep is a lot harder. Routines are best for sleeping so try to get to sleep before 10.30 pm each night, so that you can start creating the hormones during the night that will help you wake up revitalised.

When your children are young, you create a bedtime ritual for them to help get them to sleep easier. Do the same for yourself. Have a set bedtime each night and in the hour before this time relax in a dark environment or a dimly lit environment and create the space where you are not thinking or working through all the problems of the day. As mums we tend to think about all the possibilities for the next day or the next week. Your busy mind is stopping you from sleeping.

If you find that your mind is busy with thoughts, write those thoughts down to come back to tomorrow. Try a guided mediation to help calm the mind and reduce extraneous thoughts. By using the recommendations in Chapter 11 and 12 you can reduce the recurrent thoughts running around in your head. If your brain continues to be switched on during the night with the loads of tasks that you need to do for the next day, then keep a pen and paper next to your bed, write these thoughts down before you go to bed so that you can rest assured you will remember them in the morning and you won't create an endless cycle going round and round in your head.

Use a beautiful Epsom salt foot bath to soak your feet for twenty minutes before you go to bed. What better relaxing activity than this can you think of? Epsom salts contain magnesium which can help you relax into sleep. You can also add lavender and chamomile essential oils for added relaxation.

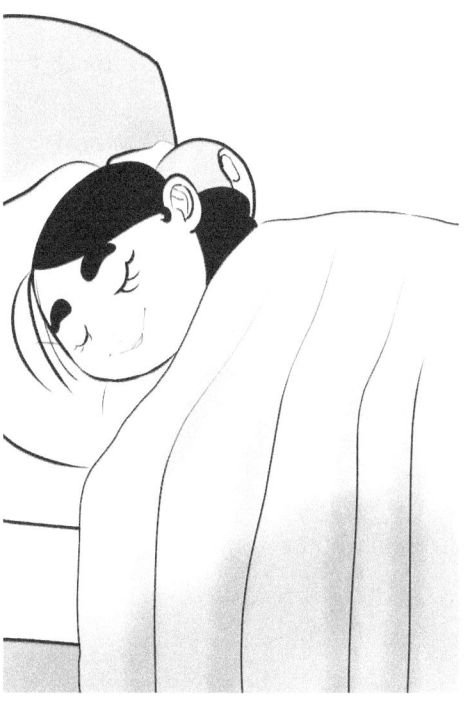

Limit any interactions with e-mails, work-related things or emotionally charged conversations with friends and family. Think about these scenarios: you are casually using your computer in bed and all of a sudden you receive an e-mail about an issue at work; or you had an emotionally charged conversation with a family member or friend before bed. Your body perceives them as stressful events. Thus, stress hormones such as adrenaline are created and this keeps you awake, ready to fight or flee.

All Night Sleep

Good quality sleep is not only about getting to sleep, but it's also about staying asleep throughout the whole night. If you're waking up during the night, it could be due to a few reasons.

Magnesium is needed for relaxation and sleep, it aids muscle and nerve relaxation and helps with the production of melatonin. Restless legs or anxious feelings during the night are a common occurrence with magnesium deficiency. If you are having trouble sleeping, get your magnesium levels checked. We have already discussed in the last chapter that a combination of blood, urine and salivary tests can show the true level of magnesium in your body.

Waking in the early hours of the morning, around 3 to 4 am, can be due to blood sugar irregularities. Eat a good quality meal for your evening dinner that involves salad or vegetables and protein. Your last meal of the day should be consumed at least two hours before bedtime. Avoid heavy, fatty or spicy foods as it can cause you to wake up during the night. Reducing the intake of processed sugar is important to help reduce the blood sugar rollercoaster. If you want sweets after dinner, choose some dates with a handful of nuts and a small amount of yoghurt or coconut yoghurt, or have baked apple with crushed nuts and seeds.

Do you often wake up between midnight and 3 am? If so, you might like to look at your liver and gall bladder functions. Your liver may be feeling overwhelmed and there are ways that we can help to clean out the liver and give you that refreshing sleep all through the night. Look at the recommendations in Chapter 2 on how you can support your liver.

Stimulants such as coffee, caffeinated drinks and nicotine can impact one's sleep. Avoid stimulants after 2 pm. While most people associate alcohol with relaxation, it can have a negative impact on your quality of sleep. Alcohol can cause you to feel hot in the early hours of the morning and interrupt your sleep.

The comfort of the bed is important. Make sure that your bed is comfortable and that the temperature is the right temperature for you – not too hot and not too cold. If your bed is too old, it might need to be replaced with a more comfortable one. Beware of latex-based beds as they can cause your body to overheat through the night and this will wake you up.

Mobile phones next to your bed can interrupt your sleep as they can vibrate and beep through the night with text messages, social media alerts and e-mails. Switch your phone to silent or better yet put the phone in another room. They radiate small amounts of Wi-Fi signal and radiation and this may impact your sleep. There is a lot of conjecture about mobile phone radiation and cancer but I, for one, don't want to wait and see the conclusive results. My personal stance is that they can contribute to chronic disease and cancer. If you are having trouble sleeping, then it's best that all mobile phones are out of the bedroom.

Are your children or animals waking you up through the night? Find ways to help them settle better so that it helps you with your sleep. I know my children sometimes have times of nightmares or restlessness and I try to identify if there's an emotional component for them or if there could be something like intestinal worms that are disrupting their sleep patterns. When they settle and sleep through the night, then you will too. Animals are a major culprit for lost sleep for some of my clients. Cats and dogs can wake you up to go out for a toilet break in early hours of the morning. I don't profess to have all the answers for this one, except to put them out for a toilet break just before your bedtime or install a doggie or cat door so they can let themselves out.

Are you a light sleeper and find that your sleep gets disrupted easily from noise? There are white noise CDs that you can play during the night to stifle out extraneous noises. If it is a partner that snores, look to get a pair of comfortable earplugs to help block out noise, or look for ways to reduce their snoring through healthy lifestyle changes.

Bright lights streaming in through your window might wake you up. If there are bright street lights outside your window or cars driving past, this could have an impact on your melatonin levels. Invest in blackout blinds or thick, heavy curtains to keep the light away so that you can sleep pleasantly through your night.

Regular daytime exercise helps with sleep regulation, but make sure your exercise is not too close to your bedtime as that can keep you awake. Some clients find that an exercise programme after they finish work is a great way to unwind. On the other hand, many clients who have trouble sleeping find that exercise after 6 pm can prevent them from sleeping at night. Find the right time that works best for you.

Start Your Sleep Pattern at the Beginning of the Day

The circadian rhythm is the biological process that drives our body through the day and night. Animals don't have watches, but they know when it is time to eat or sleep as part of their natural rhythm. Take cows for instance, I grew up on acreage, and the cows would always start to wander over the milking shed before they were rounded up. They would stand there and wait for the farmer to open the gates for them to go into the shed. This was due to their circadian rhythm.

Enhance your own circadian rhythm by going to bed at the same time each night but more importantly getting up at the same time each day. When you do wake up, go outside and expose your eyes to sunlight first thing in the morning without sunglasses. We usually get up and get ready to hop in our car with our sunglasses on and then go into our office and stay in the house all day where we have artificial light. By exposing your eyes to natural sunlight at the beginning of the day, it can help to establish the correct cortisol and melatonin rhythm.

Herbs can be useful for helping correct sleep patterns for those who have trouble sleeping despite putting in good sleeping practices. The herbs I use regularly in my clinic that can help to reduce anxiety and promote relaxation into sleep, including Passionflower, Zizyphus, Skullcap, Magnolia and Valerian. Consult with a qualified herbalist to find out which of these herbs would be best used in your situation as some herbs can interact with other medications.

In my clinic, there are some mums who simply say that they cannot get the nine hours of sleep they need as they just don't get everything done while the kids are awake. My first suggestion is for them to record everything that they are doing and see what activity is non-essential that could be removed from the day to give them more time for sleep. If there is a legitimate reason for a lesser number of hours of sleep, such as they work night shifts and have children that rise early in the morning, then focusing on sleep of shorter duration but better in quality is the next step. Implementing the tips that I have suggested in this chapter will help create that good quality sleep.

Your Action Plan

Establish a good bedtime routine with some dim lights and low stimulation in your room. Make the bedtime the same time every night. Keep your mobile phone out of your bedroom and take off any Fitbit or wireless devices that you might be wearing that send signals back to your phone as these digital devices can interfere with your sleep.

Have a good quality dinner at least two hours before bed and make it predominantly vegetables or salad, with good quality protein. Avoid heavy, fatty meals, highly sugary meals and snacks, also avoid caffeine and alcohol.

This action plan will help to create the ideal environment for you to get good quality sleep and wake up refreshed and invigorated the next day.

10. Recharge ME

'I believe that the greatest gift you can give your family and the world is a healthy you.'

– Joyce Meyer

I find that many women, especially mums, tend to put themselves last. They are so busy looking after their children, being a wife, a mother, working and tending to all the daily household chores that they tend to forget to take time for themselves and recharge. All of their energy is invested into everyone and everything else – they don't have time or energy for themselves.

Whilst this book is aimed at mums, it is not only mums that these concepts apply to. These principles can be used by all. In this current age of modern technology where we are always plugged into e-mails, social media and phone calls, we can find it hard to switch off. We are on constant demand. This places us in a space where the body constantly produces stress hormones and uses its vital nutrients faster than can be replenished.

Think of the role of a mum in terms of a wagon wheel. At the centre of the wagon wheel is a cog. This is important to the function of the wagon wheel. Everything spins around it. When the wagon wheel turns it spins around the cog. If one of the spokes that radiate from the cog breaks, the wheel will still keep turning. Whereas if that centre cog falls apart, everything else will fall apart with it. The mums are the centre cog and they drive the wheel. The spokes of the wheel can be likened to the everyday roles that mums do – the family members, the job or career, the friends and the household duties. One spoke can fall out and the rest will still continue to spin. If the mum falls apart, it feels as if everything will fall apart as well.

Taking time out for yourself will help you solidify your place as the cog in the centre of that wheel. From my experience, I find that many mums feel guilty if they take time out for themselves, this guilt drives them to keep going despite feeling depleted or fatigued. It is important to remember that you will be better able to be there for others when you look after your own health and vitality.

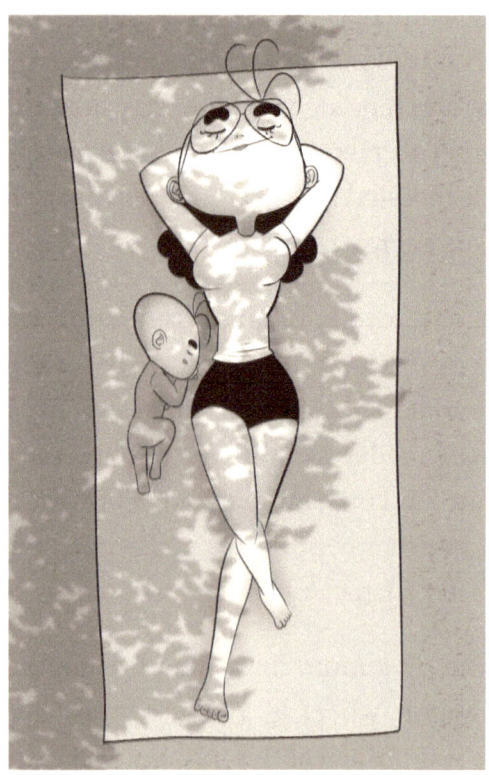

What Is Recharging?

When I talk about recharging I'm talking about rest, relaxation and fun; creating a space where your body can stop producing stress chemicals and rushing through the day; just relax, be present and be in the moment. The type of recharging moment can be whatever it is that you love to do. Find an activity that at the end of it you think, 'Wow, I needed that, I feel good now.'

The aim of the recharge time is to create a space where you step out of the everyday demands of your life. At this point in time you are doing something for yourself that boosts your mood, helps you feel relaxed and forget the grind of daily tasks for the duration of the recharge time.

Examples of some recharging activities that my clients enjoy include:

- walking along the beach
- sitting on the beach watching waves roll in
- painting or other craft activities
- reading a good book
- a massage
- meditation class
- yoga class
- having a cup of tea while watching the sunset
- playing a musical instrument
- some clients just want to sit still and listen to their favourite music without being interrupted

What would your recharge time consist of?

When you take time for yourself, you re-energise yourself. Just as you recharge your phone at the end of the day, your body needs time to recharge. When you consistently take time to recharge, you will feel more relaxed and able to cope with your daily tasks. You create feel-good hormones called endorphins. These are the opposite to your stress hormones and they help you feel invigorated, joyful and happy again.

Taking time to recharge may seem like you are wasting time or letting others down, but by giving your body time to recharge you will begin to enjoy life again, you will feel more in control of your life have better moods and feel less anxiety on a daily basis. When you take time for yourself and recharge, you will be more capable to be there when your family and work need you.

How Recharge Time Helps Reduce Frazzle and Fatigue

One reason for fatigue can be due to the fact that we're always turned on. Women have many roles to play in this present day. Gone are the days of just tending to the family and the house without any worries and without any extra demands. In this modern age of living, we're on call 24/7 dealing with multiple demands of the modern mum.

We constantly feel a perception of stress stemming from financial issues, relationship issues, health issues, our loved ones, work stresses, even our own appearance and our own thoughts. We get consumed by this continual bombardment of potential stresses. If these stresses were a tiger, then it would seem that we were constantly being chased and we need an unlimited amount of energy to run away from that tiger.

Recharge time allows you to step out from these constant demands for a moment and stop the stress merry-go-round in your body.

Let's look at recurrent negative thoughts and how recharge time will help to stop them from robbing you of your energy. In Chapter 7, I discussed how negative thoughts are energy robbers. Thoughts about how bad our life is, that the boss isn't being nice to us, that we hate the traffic that's on the way to work, the children's misbehaviours, or a relationship issue, all add to your stress response and they drain your energy. There are repetitive negative thoughts happening to us every day and they can carry us away into an environment where we feel fatigued, overwhelmed, unmotivated and unable to cope.

Part of the reason to utilise recharge time is so that you can put these negative thoughts aside for a moment and boost your mood. Many times you feel so relaxed afterward that you forget to pick back up those negative thoughts at the end of the recharge time.

To turn off the stress response, and to turn off the crazy thoughts that are going through your mind every day, we need to have techniques or routines that we do to help us switch off in this crazy world.

I find that some of my clients have long-term stress and accept this as normal. For instance, I had a client who had been working in a stressful workplace with long hours; bullying and intimidation were prevalent, and this had been happening for three years. Due to the length of time and the amount of stress, she thought her level of stress was normal. Her body showed symptoms of chronic stress – she was having trouble sleeping, and when she did sleep she was dreaming about what she had to do at work the next day. Anxiety started as soon as she woke up thinking about work and she thought about work well into the evening. It was impacting other aspects of her life and the life of her family.

As part of her health assessment, her adrenal hormones were tested. Her cortisol levels were imbalanced, instead of fluctuating as they should. The treatment that I recommended included her learning how to disconnect from the work place issues. She needed to create a routine that helped her disengage from her work issues.

We discussed activities and routines that could be created to help her leave work at work and create time for herself at the end of the day and then time for her family. The activity that my client opted for was a fifteen minute walk along the beach after work before she got home to her family. This allowed her to reset herself and get centred and release all the work pressures before she went home and dealt with her family and the rest of the things that needed to go on that day.

Initially she felt she was letting her family down but only after a couple of weeks, she felt more balanced, was sleeping better and was better able to deal with the challenges of work. While her energy was still not 100%, she felt that the quality time to recharge herself gave her more energy throughout the day.

Find Your Way to Stop the Cycle of Exhaustion

Many women need to work for financial or personal reasons, and they still have to take care of the family and do all the other maternal roles on top of their work. Most of my clients will have at least some level of exhaustion because they are doing all of their roles well into the night after the family have gone to bed, then they fall into bed exhausted, only to wake up the next day and do it all over again.

Take time to recharge, stop this cycle and allow yourself to take a moment that refreshes you.

The first thing to do is to find an activity that you love to do every day. It doesn't have to be an hour-long project if you are short on time – although an hour would be amazing. If you are really time poor, start with five to ten minutes. Look at some of the activities we listed above for inspiration. To help identify a client's Recharge ME activity, I ask them about their hobbies or interests. Look to activities that inspire or excite you.

Wanting a quick fix to get the effects of Recharge ME Time? Look at something that makes you laugh. Laughter has been shown to be very beneficial to the body. It stimulates the intake of your oxygen and improves your circulation, it increases endorphins – the feel-good hormone – decreases your stress response and stimulates your muscle relaxation. Laughter will fast track the effects of your Recharge ME Time and stop the cycle of negative thoughts and stress hormones and elevate your mood, leaving you feeling relaxed and more able to deal with everyday tasks.

Find a television comedy sitcom that you can laugh at for fifteen to twenty minutes. Find a photo that has a funny memory attached to it so that when you look at it you giggle every time. Share a laugh with some friends. Find a joke book and read some old jokes. You could even look on YouTube for funny videos of animals and their antics to help make you laugh.

You could also spend time watching children play. Little children get up to so many antics, it's lovely to watch them and they can easily trigger your laughter. My kids love to do things to make my husband and I laugh. It seems like a mission or a competition for them to see who gets the most laughs. Remember, it's not about laughing at children or other people, but laughing with them and how much they're enjoying their lives.

Find something that creates laughter and schedule that into something that you can do regularly.

If you don't have a hobby or interest, then include meditation or mindfulness routines into your daily schedule. Incorporating a meditation into your day will help you relax and stop the thoughts from running through your mind, and it can also help to identify your goals and life path. Meditation can start with just ten minutes or even go up to an hour.

There are some people that have difficulty meditating – they can't sit in the meditative space without the mind getting cluttered with thoughts. If you find it hard to meditate then use a guided meditation that helps you focus on a voice, this can help to reduce those circling thoughts that are rotating through your mind every day. There are many apps available that provide this service – one that I recommend is *Headspace*. It is good to do these before bed to help you relax into sleep.

If you don't have time for a full meditation, then take ten minutes to connect with your body. Feel where the tension is in your body, feel what your toes feel like. What about your nose, how does that feel? Feel how your heart is beating. If during this process your thoughts get you off-track, then relax and just go back to focusing on breathing. It does take practice to do this without any runaway thoughts, but it will happen with practice.

If you are still thinking you really don't have time for meditation or to sit and feel the tension in your body, then use the following technique to calm and reset your body. This is a technique that I get many of my clients to do, and it only takes one minute.

Firstly, you stop what you're doing. If you're at work, go to the bathroom or you close the door of your office. If you are at home with the family then go to your bedroom and close the door.

This process involves taking six slow, deep breaths over one minute. Inhale for five seconds, then exhale while counting from one to five. Inhale again for five seconds, and then exhale for another five seconds. Repeat this four more times. At the end of this small exercise, be aware of how your body feels. Is there any tension left, is your mind still racing? The process of concentrating on counting each five seconds helps to stop and slow the mind. The deeper, slower breaths help to oxygenate the body and create a relaxed environment.

The more often you do this, the easier this exercise will become, and it will become part of your daily regime. You could set your phone to do this time-out technique every hour. You take a minute out of every hour just to get into the habit of doing this where you take a few deep breaths, you stop what you're doing, relax, centre yourself and then you can go back to the tasks you were doing before, and you will feel less pressured, more energised and more able to cope in those situations.

Another technique that can be used as part of your Recharge ME Time – and this is a great way to switch off those negative thoughts – is to keep a journal to record all the positive things going on in your life. Gratitude journals are a great way to retrain your mind to look for the good things in life and this will help to improve your outlook on life. You could take five minutes at the end of the day to write down all the good things that occurred that day. There are apps that you can use to help with this. I use *Write A Day* where I record all the positive things that are going on in my day. You can add photos to your entries as well. This will help you to concentrate on the good things in life and help you to recharge.

I find that when I talk with the fatigued mums that visit my clinic about the Recharge ME process, many of them have feelings of guilt for putting themselves first. It's okay for you to take time for yourself, just explain to your family or to your loved ones that you're simply taking time to recharge yourself. Clarify with them that when you take time for yourself you will feel better, relaxed and more able to cope with life's demands.

Remember that it is okay to take time for yourself and to reward yourself. It is okay not to have to answer your e-mails, your phones, or your texts immediately. Let the person leave a message and you will get back to them when the time is right for you. It is okay to say no to someone who requests your time if you're unable to do it without exhausting yourself and it is okay for things to not be perfect at that time. It's okay to tell other people how you feel. It's okay to acknowledge and ask for help. It is okay to just stop, rest and rejuvenate to restore your energy.

Action Time – Start Small and Build Up

If you're thinking, 'Oh, I don't have time for this, I don't have time to go for a walk on the beach', or 'I don't have time to do a yoga class', start with something small, start with something that will only take up five to ten minutes. It might be a piece of music, or an audiobook, or just going out and standing on the grass in the sunlight, breathing in that fresh air.

Build this up as you feel your energy change and as you feel more in control. You're worth it to take that time for you.

The takeaway message for you to do right now is make a date with yourself and make it regular. Find a hobby that interests you and invigorates you and do it regularly and enjoy every minute of it without guilt.

11. Game Plan

'If you keep good food in your fridge, you will eat good food.'

– Errick McAdams

Have you ever felt like there's a mountain of tasks to do and you don't know which one to start first? Do you get home feeling tired and fatigued at the end of the day after work or after chasing the kids around and wonder what to cook?

A Game Plan will help you maximise your time and make good food choices for you and your family's health. Being organised and eating right will then help to improve your energy and reduce your sense of being overwhelmed.

What is a Game Plan?

Planning your meals each week or fortnight will help you plan, not only what you are cooking, but also your shopping list. This saves sanity, time, money and reduces food wastage.

When you are already fatigued and strained from your day, the last thing you want to consider is what to feed the family tonight and how you are going to summon the energy to make that meal.

This is when many people tend to go for a quick solution such as takeaway or other non-nutritious meals.

Adopting the habit of planning your meals will help you take charge and you will be able to make extra meals for those leftover lunches or dinners and this will feel like a blessing.

There is a common misconception that making healthy, nutritious meals is time-consuming. It doesn't have to be at all. Meal planning helps make sure you are prepared with the ingredients needed and if there is some preparation needed such as soaking nuts or making part of the meal another day. You will find it easier to plan them into your week with a meal plan.

In doing this, my clients find that they are less likely to reach for those energy robbing fast food meals and that they can easily fuel their bodies with amazing, nutritionally rich foods.

Think of this scenario, it's 5 pm on a busy weekday night, you're hungry, tired and exhausted from the demands of your work. The kids are hungry and grizzly, they start fighting and get the 'hangries'. You have to make something for dinner but because of the fatigue you can't quite decide what you're going to make or how you're going to make the dish with the remaining energy you have left. As you get ready to prepare something, you find that you are missing ingredients that you need to make the meal.

You now have another decision to make – do you go to the shops to get the missing ingredients, which takes up more precious time and energy, or do you decide to just open a packet of noodles for the kids or go to the local fast food outlet and grab something quick, yet nutritionally poor?

I don't know about you, but I find this scenario very draining and I have been there in the past.

Let's think of another alternative for you.

You get home from a hectic day at work and you are tired but because you spent fifteen minutes on Sunday planning your meals, you already know what is going to be cooked. Instead of needing to make another decision with a foggy head, you just go about preparing the meal, as if you are on autopilot. There are no major decisions to be made when you are already feeling fatigued. The kids already anticipate what's for dinner as they have seen your meal plan.

Maybe you feel too tired to cook at all tonight. But because you have planned your meals, you know that there is a premade meal leftover in the freezer from a couple of nights ago. This meal is nutritious and just needs to be heated up and served. It's quick, easy and you feel empowered, instead of feeling more drained by the process.

Meal planning actually helps to reduce the stress and helps you to keep in control of what's going on.

Advantages of Meal Planning

To create sustained energy and be able to cope with the demands of daily life of a mother, we need to eat nutritious foods. When you are fatigued, and already low on energy, meal preparation tends to suffer. When we are short on time, it's a reflex to go for quick, easy meals. Those quick, easy meals are not always nutritious.

Another issue with being fatigued and hungry is that choices are made to go for food that give a quick energy burst. These choices tend to be energy robbing foods such as sugar and alcohol, or you may choose mass-produced fast foods, which have little to no nutritional value at all, and then ultimately end up depleting more of your energy. Eating the right food helps the probiotic gut flora

– levels of the gut flora has been linked to moods, including the reduction of anxiety and depression.

By being organised, you can choose and plan meals that fit your weekly schedule and time frame, which will more likely to be nutritious. Meal planning will maximise your time, reduce your effort and improve your energy. This takes away any decision fatigue and any time wasted standing in front of your fridge or your cupboard wondering what ingredients there are to make a meal and wondering how you're going to have enough energy to create this meal.

The How-To of Meal Planning

Let's look at meal planning and how you can do it for yourself and your family. Firstly, set aside a time to plan your meals. You might pick a day or a time of the week where you are relaxed and a time that you have energy. It may be a Sunday morning after you've had your breakfast, it could be a Saturday afternoon after you've spent the day with your family and you're feeling good about what's going on.

Everyone is different, so selecting a time when you are not rushed and you are clear-headed is best. Once you have the routine of meal planning down pat you will find that it becomes quicker.

Meal planning itself only takes about ten to twenty minutes and it is the foundation to supply your body with the nutrients so that you can create sustained energy for the whole week.

The more you do meal planning, the easier it will become, and it will take less time each time you do it. To help you start, create your own or download a meal template. This template could be laminated and written on with a whiteboard marker so that you can wipe off each week to be filled in again for the next week.

Visit my website *www.teressatodd.com* to download a template for your use. Go to resources tab and use code word FABULOUS for access.

After you've set aside some time to do your meal plan, go to your fridge and pantry and look at the foods and ingredients you have. This way you can use recipes that utilise the ingredients that you already have in stock.

Plan ahead. Choose recipes that can be doubled in quantity, this way you can freeze portions for future dinners or use leftovers for lunches for the next day. You could increase the vegetable content on the meal to ensure the nutritional quantity. This also ensures it is more cost effective than if you were to just increase the quantity of meats.

When you create meals to be frozen, make sure that you label and date the meals, so you know what they are and when they were prepared. This will help reduce any surprises when you defrost something that you forgot you had.

Look for meal ideas and inspiration. You can use cookbooks that you already have for recipe ideas. A cookbook that may help to get you started is *No Time to Cook* by Donna Hay. There is a helpful chapter called 'Some Now Some Later'. The recipes in this section are specific for freezing. From a nutritional standpoint I would like to see you add more vegetables or have a premade salad to accompany many of the dishes to increase the phytochemical and vitamin-mineral intake.

Looking for meal ideas online? There is a plethora of websites with healthy recipes. I will look through websites and if a recipe interests me, I simply save the recipe for the next week's planning. Generally, I don't spend time looking for ideas but instead save them as I come across them while looking at other things. This way I have a folder of recipes for when I need something that my family hasn't had before. Pinterest and Facebook are good sites to help you find recipes. Even your favourite chef will have recipes available online.

Whatever the recipe is that you use, just ensure that it is loaded with salad or vegetables. If the recipes are predominantly meat-based, then add extra vegetables or include a salad with that meal as I have suggested with the Donna Hay's recipes. Vegetarian meals may not need to be increased in content unless you are doubling the quantity for freezing.

There are apps available to help select and store recipes, as well as create shopping lists to save you more time. Apps that I recommend are *Mealime* and *Yummly*. Each of these apps help you construct and customise the meals while incorporating different eating styles and allergy requirements. You can then use the generated shopping lists to help you shop and save time.

I use a website called *Cookidoo*. This site is for those who have a Thermomix. The website allows you to plan your meals and generate a shopping list, and the added advantage of this is that the recipes can be synced to your Thermomix device if you have the Thermomix Cook-Key. The Thermomix will then take you through the steps of the recipe and do the cooking for you. Personally, I find this device saves me a lot of time as I can spend time with my children – helping with their homework, or help them get showered, or do their lunches for the next day – while the Thermomix cooks. This is my idea of multitasking.

Thermomix and Tefal Cuisine Companion are all-in-one thermal cooking machines. They perform a variety of functions in just one device. They chop, whip, mix, knead, steam, blend, stir, whisk, mill and cook to precise temperatures. These devices come with cook books, have online recipes and many unofficial online groups to share recipes. Because the thermal cooking devices do much of the chopping and cooking for you, it can help reduce active cooking time and clean up time. There is an upfront cost to these devices, but you will save money in the long-term as they can reduce the cost of groceries when you make many meals from scratch with natural, unprocessed ingredients.

If you're still thinking, 'I don't know what to cook, I don't know how to meal plan', visit *www.teressatodd.com* and download the 7-day meal plan. This has a variety of nutritious meals to help get you started. Go to resources tab and use code word FABULOUS for access.

Helpful Tips for Meal Planning

When choosing meals for your weekly meal plan. Look at meals that are family favourites and include them in your plan. Your family favourites could be a satay chicken dish, a curry dish or a pasta dish. Include one or two of them each week and rotate them over the next month. Make double batches of these for when you are time poor and low on energy. You may have a night in the week that you get home late from work or the kids have after-school activities that run till late. You can then whip the leftovers of these family favourites out, reheat and *voilà* – dinner is done.

When you are planning your meals, look at what lunch box ideas you could do at the same time. For instance, if you are making a salad to go with dinner, you could make extra for a salad for the next day's lunch, or you could incorporate ingredients from the salad into a wrap. This will save you time, especially if it's for your children's lunches. It doesn't take much extra time and effort to chop or prepare what you are already doing for dinner.

Another tip is to reuse previous meal plans. Create copies of your meal plans then you can rotate them over the next few months and reduce your plan time even more.

Still Feeling Time Poor?

Invest in a slow cooker. Slow cookers cook the food for you while you are working or sleeping. Slow cookers are a great way of making a lot of different meals, with very little effort. They help increase the quantities of meals for freezing.

One of my clients allocates one day a week to do her slow cooking. She has a couple of slow cookers and cooks a different meal in each one at the same time. They are left to cook during the day when she is spending time with her family on a Sunday. Then she divides the dishes up and freezes them for meals during the week. She is optimising her time as it doesn't take that much longer to chop for two slow cookers than it is to chop for one.

Plan to have one day where you have a big cook up where you make several meals for the next week and then freeze them for later use. Many of my clients find that this helps them during the week when they run short on time. Involve your family or friends to help. I do this during winter with my mother-in-law. We choose one Sunday a month to cook up large batches of soup and make six to eight frozen meals for each family.

You can invite over friends or family that do not live with you for a cook up. One of my clients has her adult son come over once a month and they spend several hours making many meals for the next month. She cherishes this time with her son as not only does she get to make meals for herself, but she also gets to spend quality time with him. Even if your children are still living at home, get them to help. This will teach them the importance of nutrition and what to do when they move out.

Another way to save time is to get involved in meal swaps with other mothers or workmates. Since cooking double batches doesn't take much longer than single batches, this is a great way to reduce your active cook time and increase the variety of your meals.

Another option that can help many time-poor mums is to get together with other mothers and create a meal swap group. Create double batches of frozen meals and then swap these with other mothers. You will find that you can enjoy meals that you may not normally make. The comradery from other mothers is a great support and will help when you are feeling tired and low. If you don't swap meals, you could swap recipe ideas or meal plans, this will reduce your workload of finding new recipes.

Action Time

Set aside fifteen to twenty minutes to create a meal plan. Choose a time that's suitable for you and when you've got energy. Create a weekly meal plan that includes meals that can be doubled – freeze half of the portion for another meal or use leftovers for lunch. Once you have planned the meals you can create a grocery list.

Plan some time to do a large scale cook up. Do this once a month and create meals that can be frozen. Connect with other mums and swap some meal ideas to increase your variety if you are wanting different meals for your family.

Planning your meals will save you time and nourish you and your family. By planning and creating a grocery list you will also save money. After you have planned your weekly or fortnightly meals and generated the grocery list, look at how you can save more time when buying groceries. For instance, use online shopping to purchase groceries and get them delivered or pick them up on the way home from work, saving you from pushing yourself to go grocery shopping when you are already tired from the day and dragging your children along too. I find I save even more money by buying online as my children are not with me asking for all kinds of foods that we don't need. Planning will also help you buy in bulk and save even more money.

Go plan your meals now and reap the rewards!

12. Take Control

'Planning is bringing the future into the present so you can do something about it now.'

– Alan Lakein

The current era pressures many women to become superwomen. For women to be able to juggle the myriad of roles that they currently try to engage in, there needs to be a strategy – a method that helps put the roles into a schedule and reduces feelings of overwhelm. The most successful working mothers are the ones that create schedules and plans for their week, month or year.

Creating set plans and scheduling your tasks allow you to take control of your life. This will reduce the impact of stress on your body and you can even allocate Recharge ME Time.

Why Plan?

In my experience, mothers are time poor and overwhelmed with the many roles that they have. This can cause frustration, guilt, stress and fatigue, to name a few.

Think about your life: How many tasks do you have to do every day? Do you find yourself thinking about these tasks constantly?

How long is your to-do list? Does your list include many of the following: children's after-school activities, what to cook for dinner, work deadlines, house cleaning, your kid's school issues, paying the bills, etc? This list of tasks and more all run around in your mind like a mouse on a spinning wheel constantly going around and around.

The body doesn't distinguish the difference between your thoughts and your reality, so in your mind, this constant to-do list is actually happening each minute every day. Your body responds as if the events are occurring. As we have already addressed in previous chapters, in response to stress the adrenals produce short bursts of stress hormones and these are beneficial only in the short-term. What happens when your thoughts are constant and unrelenting, remembering all the tasks that you have to do each day? When overwhelming thoughts continue day in and day out, it contributes to feeling depleted and tired. Your cells produce energy in response and the adrenals continually create stress hormones, long-term fatigue will set in. This sequence of events occurs even if the thoughts are only in your mind and not physically occurring.

A thought triggers an emotion and this emotion triggers a physical response. There is a saying 'You are what you eat'. Similarly, your thoughts become you. As Buddha said, 'The mind is everything. What you think, you become.'

Let's prove this concept. Have you ever thought about a loved one and then felt the emotion of that love and your heart flutters a little bit, or your breaths quicken? Do this now, think about someone you love, your kids or your partner for instance. Feel what goes on in your body. Do you feel a warm glow, does your heart rate increase, do you feel almost euphoric? The response that you are feeling in your body is happening because of the thought and therefore the emotion.

The next exercise to do is to think about something you do that you dread, or you hate doing. It might be speaking in public or taking an exam – something that you immensely dislike. Emotions will be stirred up when you think of these scenarios. Now feel what happens. Does your chest tighten? Does your heart race a little bit? Again, your body has responded to the thoughts of the brain, you actually didn't do that exam or speak in public, you just thought about it and yet your body reacted to it. This is how thoughts can trigger physiological reactions in your body.

Now expand the concept. If you're thinking about all of those tasks that you have to do every day and you have all of those thoughts revolving around in your head about things that you dread, or a conversation you need to have, then you will be creating a physical response in the body, this response will lead you to feel tired, fatigued and worn out.

Do you find yourself constantly thinking about things that you have to do tomorrow, next week or next month? Do you have endless to-do lists? Many of my clients say, 'I've got to-do lists and I feel more overwhelmed and more fatigued'. To-do lists can create a situation where you feel paralysed by overwhelm. You see the number of tasks on that to-do list and then think about how much time it will all take. I know I have personally written many to-do lists and I even had to-do lists that are many pages long. I always felt overwhelmed with my lists as they kept growing and I didn't seem to get on top of them. I would put off the really hard tasks, or I would find that one task would take twice as long as it should have.

Do you get side-tracked in between tasks? Emails and social media alerts are the worst offenders for side-tracking you from your current task. The phone notifications come in constantly and then we stop the current task to check those e-mails or alerts and get side-tracked, eventually we don't get to finish that task.

When you have a schedule or have planned your time for every day of the week, you can use this to keep all your current tasks in order, instead of juggling several things at once. Schedule time for e-mails, social media, after-school activities, work tasks, cleaning your house and cooking dinner. Scheduling will help you take control of your life and regain your energy and vigour.

What would happen if you were able to stop the mouse's spinning wheel and just be in the present moment, not thinking about the tasks that are needed to be done? Would you feel at ease and more empowered if you had the day planned and you were able to move from one task to another without the extra pressure of remembering what to do next?

The How-To of Making a Strategy

Planning your day helps stop the uncontrollable spinning mouse wheel of thoughts.

Plan your day before it starts. Allocate time in a relaxed setting to define your day. Perhaps set aside some time in the evening to plan your next day. The flow-on effect is to rid your mind of the recurrent to-do list and help you establish restful sleep. Recording your tasks and allocating a set time to do each task will free up your mind and many tasks will become automatic. You will get into a routine and go from one task to the next without any decision fatigue or wasting time thinking what you should do next.

As you get into the rhythm of planning you will find that you can plan a full week or a month, with some flexibility for pop-up events that occur with your kids.

To do this: Set aside time and space to do your tasks and allocate time for all the duties in your day – your morning routine, exercise time, dinner preparation time, work and time for the kids. Planning is simply allocating time for each of your tasks for the day rather than writing a long list of things to do and never quite getting through them. Many successful people do this, but for busy mums it will help remove constant thoughts that stop you from living in the moment. You will even find that your energy is more stable.

Creating plans helps you to take charge. You'll be able to create a space that allows you to get all of your tasks done and you can stop worrying about the little things you haven't done yet. You can rest easy and go to sleep at night knowing that the next day will flow and you will have enough time for all your tasks.

One thing to remember is to not overload your time planner. Be real and allow sufficient time to complete each task. If you don't allow enough time, it will reinforce your stressed state and continue the fatigue and overwhelmed state. If you finish a task really early, then you can reward yourself with a well-earned break. Go and sit outside, have a cup of tea and just feel how good it is to have all the jobs done. Or you could tick off another job and get ahead of your schedule.

Advantages of Time Planning

Time planning not only completes the myriad of tasks in your day, but your family will be able to see your schedule. Maybe they will even help out (*hint hint, kids*).

The main advantage of scheduling and time planning is that you will be able to schedule time and relaxation for yourself instead of working furiously late into the evening catching up on things after the kids have gone to bed. Meal preparation, regular exercise and Recharge ME Time can be planned. This alleviates the 'I don't have time' factor that mums often have.

Many mums come to me and say, 'I just don't have time to exercise and I don't have time to sit and relax', they feel overwhelmed and this contributes to their fatigue. Scheduling time for yourself will give you something to look forward to each day. Your energy levels will be more consistent because you can plan your day around your energy. Choose to accomplish jobs that require more mental activity at a time when you feel more energised.

We all have the same amount of time each day. It is just how we use it that makes us different.

My role as a health professional is to help clients move from where they are in life to a point that generates health and well-being. When I go through and work out a schedule for them or plan out what their priorities are and allocate time for it, they are able to take charge. When they do that they can sleep better, because if they're worried about all of the things that have to be done for the day, they have trouble switching off and would lie awake at night thinking about all the tasks for the next day.

Jane, a mum of two, came to my clinic feeling tired and run-down. She told me that at the end of the day, she would just flop into bed absolutely exhausted. After the kids went to bed, she would continue attending to more tasks, including the washing, cleaning the house, or checking e-mails for work before the next day. Even though she was exhausted, when she got to bed she would have trouble switching off to go to sleep. Her brain was still wired and thinking about what else had to be done the next day, or what she had forgotten to do today. It would take a couple of hours to establish sleep. If she woke during the night, she struggled to get back to sleep because she was already thinking of the next day.

As part of her treatment, alongside correcting her nutrition, I discussed with her the need to be able to turn the brain off. Part of this would be to find a way to help her workload and constant thoughts. I encouraged her to create a time planner whereby at the beginning of the week she would create a plan for the week and allocate set times for her tasks including sleep, exercise time and family time. She wrote down in her diary everything that needed to be done and allocated a time slot for each activity. During this process Jane was encouraged to ask her family for help in doing some of the smaller jobs.

Following this process and correcting her nutrition, Jane found that she was no longer tackling an endless number of jobs and her mind stopped racing. Her energy and mood improved. She felt like she became her 'old self' again.

You might be thinking to yourself, 'I don't have time to plan.' As with anything new, it will take a little bit of time to start with, but it will save you time and help restore your energy in the long run.

Once this routine becomes a habit, it will take less time to plan and you will eventually have more time throughout each day.

Some clients feel that they will lose their spontaneity when they plan. It is important to plan yet keep flexibility. Plan your daily tasks and leave time for last minute family issues or friends that seem to always pop up. I know for myself that there are always things that crop up unexpectedly. If there is a day where the unexpected happens, I work with the unexpected issue, then try to work through the rest of my week where I can alter tasks and still accomplish what is needed. I never plan weekends and instead go with the flow on those days. This is part of ME time as I love spending time with my kids and my husband.

If you want a template to start yourself off with planning, visit *www.teressatodd.com* to download an example of a time planner. Go to resources tab and use the code word FABULOUS for access.

Many yearly diaries can be used to do this exercise. I recommend looking for a diary that has fifteen minute intervals rather than hourly intervals. This allows you to divide tasks up easier.

There are many apps available that you can add to your smartphone. These apps can keep you flowing through the day. They are versatile as many can sync to a computer as well as a mobile device. The advantage of an app over a diary or paper system is that you can schedule recurring tasks to recur the same time each week or month and this will also save you time re-entering or rewriting it.

When this is all done you will find that you have got more time, more energy and better ability to switch off at night, ensuring you feeling energised for the next day.

Take Control Action Plan

Get a diary (electronic or paper based) that has a day to a page so that you can allocate each of your tasks daily. Be mindful to not overload the day. Start by setting your wake up time and your morning routine. Then block out your sleep time and remember to keep the hour before bed for the bedtime routine process that we have discussed previously. Then with the rest of the day allocate your work hours and schedule in your other tasks – picking up kids, washing, cleaning, groceries, social time, time for e-mails and social media ... whatever your tasks are. They will vary from day-to-day and week-to-week.

Remember to include your Recharge ME Time.

It will take a little bit of time to get in the groove of doing this, but it will help you overcome any overwhelming feelings and take charge of your life again. If you have not done this before start by planning the next day, then you can move on to plan each week, then each month.

Get your family involved and show them your schedule. In doing this they can be mindful of your time and can help your schedule run smoother.

Afterword

Congratulations and thank you for reading this book and wanting to make changes in your life. As a mother, it can be a challenge to keep on top of all the roles that you have while keeping your energy up. I'm here to tell you it can be done!

My role as a naturopath is a privilege that allows me to help others in their health journey. Thank you for letting me be part of yours. I find it empowering that so many are able to harness their own health by making a few changes in their life. You can do this too.

Your life is the sum of all your behaviours and habits. Making change in your life starts with changing behaviours and therefore habits. Many of your current behaviours that have contributed to your current health are just habits from your life.

The good news is that habits can be changed. All it takes is to start by choosing a habit to change and then reminding yourself regularly to help reinforce that change. Take a task such as driving your car, you get in your car and put your seat belt on for safety and then start the car. While you do it automatically now, initially you had to be reminded to do each of these actions. Now, it is a habit.

Each of the areas that have been addressed in this book can become habits. Cooking larger batches of food to freeze or opting for a healthy snack and glass of water instead of a glass of wine, will become a habit. Planning your meals and weekly tasks will become a habit and you will find that you look forward to the time and energy that you save doing this.

After reading this book, select one or two areas to implement each week and the repetition of these will become a habit. As you go through this process you will discover renewed energy, vitality and patience.

Tools to help you in your process are available on my website *www.teressatodd.com*. Go to resources tab and use the code word FABULOUS for access.

Congratulations again on choosing to make a change that will not only help you to be fabulous again, but ultimately help your family. *Well done!*

Offers

1. Energy Solution Tools

Claim the templates discussed in this book including your bonus 7-day meal plan, a 'done for you' meal plan that is suited to time poor mums. This meal plan includes meals that are based on salad, fruit and vegetables as the hero of your plate. Healthy snack options are also included. Follow the meal plan to reduce your decision fatigue or select your favourite meals and add them into the meal plan template.

Go to *www.teressatodd.com* click on the resources tab and use the code word 'FABULOUS' for access.

2. Online Course Available

This online course covers each of the areas that lead to fatigue and how you can take control and correct these areas to go from frazzled and fatigued to fabulous.

Visit *www.teressatodd.com* for details of the online programme and use the code 'BOOK50' in the discount code section to get 50% off.

3. Workshop

Gain added knowledge into why you are tired and fatigued with Teressa's workshops.

Topics covered include:

- Nutrition essentials and how to ditch the diet
- Planning your time and easy tips to take control
- How to beat the subclinical, latent or stealth infections
- Detoxifying in a toxic world
- Support your adrenals, thyroid and filters
- Juggling made easy

Go to *www.teressatodd.com* for a list of dates of workshops available.

About the Author

Teressa Todd has always had an interest in helping people live a healthier life. She has two university qualifications; the first is Bachelor of Applied Science with a double major in Biochemistry and Microbiology, and a sub-major in Nutrition. Then she followed her heart to Naturopathy, attending Southern Cross University to complete her bachelor's degree in Naturopathy, making her the first university-qualified naturopath, nutritional biochemist, and microbiologist in Australia.

Naturopathy made sense to Teressa as it combines how the physical body works, how food affects us, and the mental influence on health.

Teressa has one goal in mind – to show you the best and easiest way to regain your energy and vitality for life. Her knowledge is grounded in science combined with natural medicine concepts.

Teressa is a speaker and author, and her naturopathic skills are sought after nationally and internationally. She has been consulting in her own clinic for over twenty years, helping thousands of clients achieve their desired healthy state. She was voted the Best Naturopath of the Gold Coast, helping to cement her as one of the leaders in her field. She has written for health magazines and lectured naturopathic students in Chemistry, Biochemistry and Nutrition.

Even though she considered herself solely as a clinician for years, she found her soulmate and started her own family with two beautiful children, giving her a more complete enjoyment of life and appreciation of mums juggling many tasks through each day.

To find out more:

Website: *www.teressatodd.com*

Facebook: *TeressaToddNaturopath*

Instagram: *@TeressaToddNaturopath*

If you wish to contact Teressa, e-mail *enquiry@teressatodd.com*.

www.ingramcontent.com/pod-product-compliance
Lightning Source LLC
Chambersburg PA
CBHW021109080526
44587CB00010B/453